# 3:12 TRANSFORMATION

# 3:12 TRANSFORMATION

God's Blueprint *of* Transformation for All

W.L. Ioerger

TATE PUBLISHING
AND ENTERPRISES, LLC

Published by Tate Publishing & Enterprises, LLC
127 E. Trade Center Terrace | Mustang, Oklahoma 73064 USA
1.888.361.9473 | www.tatepublishing.com

Tate Publishing is committed to excellence in the publishing industry. The company reflects the philosophy established by the founders, based on Psalm 68:11,
*"The Lord gave the word and great was the company of those who published it."*


*Cover design by Rtor Maghuyop*
*Interior design by Jomar Ouano*

Published in the United States of America

ISBN: 978-1-62510-877-7
1. Religion / Christian Ministry / Counseling & Recovery
2. Religion / Christian Life / General
13.01.18

"He who overcomes, I will make him a pillar in the temple of My God, and he shall go out no more."

—Revelation 3:12

# CONTENTS

# ACKNOWLEDGMENTS

God has blessed my wife and I with many wonderful new friends during my personal transformation, the development of 3:12 Transformation Ministry, and the writing of *3:12 Transformation* the book. Friends that have shared with us, strengthened us, and prayed with us in everyday life. We are positive this was God's hand guiding His message into the hearts and lives of others that will protect and love 3:12 Transformation and God's message, just as we have. I would like to acknowledge some of those friends at this time.

Doug C.: There was a season in my life when you were the only human I knew who could give me any hope for the future. Thank you, my friend, for your words and kindness.

Pastor Tom Zobrist: You were the vessel God chose to reveal the power of truth through Jesus Christ for my spiritual eyes to see. Thank you for your obedience to God's calling in your life.

Pastor Jeff and Monna Rasanen: God promises us shepherds to lead His sheep and tend His flocks. My family is truly blessed that you, Pastor Jeff, are the shepherd God has provided. I am also grateful in Christ for you as my friend and thankful for all the support and encouragement you have given this ministry and my spirit! Monna, thank you for being an example of love, gentleness, and encouragement for not only my wife to know, but for all the other women you influence for Christ. We love you both.

Larry Shonk: God pointed me to you early on when developing the vision 3:12 Transformation into a ministry. Thank you, my brother, for your spiritual insight, wisdom, vision, and being my partner in ministry and friend in life.

Pastor Larry and Linda McKinney: Thank you both for your heart for Jesus. You are the example of Christ that the entire world needs to see. We have been blessed by your friendship and the opportunities God has presented through it. Praise God for you both!

All our church family: Thank you all for your support, encouragement, prayers, time spent together, and above all your love. We look forward to many years of sharing life in Christ with you all. We love you.

Dr. Richard Tate and Tate Publishing: Bless you for your obedience to God's calling and the spreading of God's message. May the blessings you have given my family with your involvement in *3:12 Transformation* be returned to you in the form of God's favor. May your involvement with the spreading of the Kingdom be mighty for God.

Teresa, my wife: God blessed me more than I could repay the day I met you. Thank you for standing by me when the world told you to run. Thank you for your love and faith. I love you, Teresa.

# INTRODUCTION

To begin with, I must give praise and thanks to my God and Savior Jesus Christ. Without whom, I would never have had the courage, faith, and love to dream of writing a book about overcoming addictions and a life burdened with shame, guilt, and despair.

Father, thank You! I pray the words in this book may give hope and faith when once there was despair and doubt. May these words give peace to lost souls that once only knew anxiety and chaos. May this book bring courage and confidence to those who had only known fear and worthlessness. Above all, Father, may the words on these pages give glory and praise to Your Son, Jesus Christ, and magnify Your holy name.

May this book be an offering to You God. May it give insight to Your true love and mercy for all those who seek Your forgiveness. May this book deliver the answer to so many of Your lost children who had sought to find the cure while entangled in sin and burdened down in bondage of addictions. Those broken people, always trying to fill our hearts with the world, and our control of the world, rather than Your indescribable love.

Father, I will reveal myself through these pages in an attempt to let all those who read them have their eyes opened and their hearts convicted by the revealing of Your Holy Spirit. My prayer would be that those who read this book will undoubtedly identify that the only true antidote to a broken life is surrendering of one self and accepting Your Son's sacrifice of love and forgiveness. May the words echo through the hearts of those who read them and shatter all chains of bondage that have constrained them from Your great love. May the once fearful, lost soul You have so mercifully chosen to spread this message truly express the transformation of a new life in Jesus Christ. May this transformation be spread throughout Your creation. Through the power of Your Holy Spirit, I pray You bring forth many more transformations for Your glory. And, Father let those who read believe!

The concept, 3:12 Transformation, was a vision communicated to me through a dream by the Holy Spirit of God on November 29, 2010. God placed a calling upon my heart for a recovery program that established one hundred percent focus and credit toward Jesus Christ. Being an alcoholic who struggled with life for more than twenty years, my heart was convicted that without Jesus Christ and the guidance of the Holy Spirit, I would never attain true joyous sobriety.

In my dream, I was speaking to another man in recovery. He said to me, “You know what to do.” Immediately, I woke up and looked directly at my alarm clock upon my nightstand. The time was 3:12 a.m. I felt wide awake and felt as if a spiritual presence communicated to me; a presence of knowledge, wisdom, and guidance. The thought, 3:12 Transformation, came to my mind and out of my lips before I could even collect any of my own thoughts. I arose from bed, and I felt I was led to look at the Gospel of John 3:12, “If you do not believe when I have told you earthly things, how will you believe when I tell you Heavenly things?”

Those were the words Jesus spoke to Nicodemus while talking with him on the subject of rebirth in the Holy Spirit. I can’t explain the overwhelming energy, love, peace, and faith that ran through my spirit when I read the verse to which I believed God was directly pointing me. I spent some time in prayer and thought, and finally, I returned to sleep well after 5:00 a.m. Later that morning, I felt I was led to go through all of the chapter 3s and verse 12s in the Bible. My wife and I discovered it was a God-given recovery program that puts the verses of the Bible into action to lead us out of bondage and disparity of life. It showed us of God’s great love for us; His mercy and patience, His understanding, His encouragement, His promise of peace and joy in this life, and His promise of our eternal life with Him in heaven.

3:12 Transformation is a four-phase application of spiritual rebirth: surrender, believe, live, and proclaim. It contains twenty-six different verses, coming from all chapter 3s and verse 12s of the Bible. After twenty years of attempting to overcome alcoholism, I had realized that merely not drinking was only a fraction of the underlining problems. Yes, we have all heard this before. What do you have when you sober up a drunken horse thief? The answer: you still have a horse thief! But something resonated deeper in my soul. I began to see that conforming, functioning, and succeeding in life was an understanding I had been given through my own expectations and the standards of others. The same inner strength and voice that was telling me the world's standards are not necessarily the guarantee to happiness was also leading me to much more than what the world had to offer. What I had been searching for was true peace, forgiveness, and confidence my failures would not be repeated.

Now, before you read another sentence, I will assure you that I am not perfect, nor do I ever expect to be. However, I will tell you of the peace and trust I have received through the true surrender of giving my life to Jesus Christ. I will tell you the circumstances Christ has overcame for me. I will tell you of hope and faith. I will tell you about my relationship with the Creator of the universe that I never thought possible! I will also tell you that God longs for that same relationship with you! It is so much more than not drinking or using. We are prisoners of sin. God will not only set you free, He will burst off the chains from upon you and take you on a journey with His Son. I will explain to you in my humble terms: 3:12 Transformation.

I will describe the way my heart felt when it had been explained to me through God's guidance and use of the scriptures. This book, *3:12 Transformation,* seemed at first obviously designed for the alcoholic and addict. But what we have discovered is the outlined transformation and program will work for any life that had not known Jesus Christ, or had turned away at some point. 3:12 Transformation will lead people to Christ and freedom! We all come from different backgrounds and circumstances. Some of us may carry the burden of being the cause of great misery and pain, while others may feel as though we had been the recipient of great, unjust treatment. We are all sinners whom need salvation. Don't look back along the way; you do not want to miss a single minute of what God has in store for you!

SURRENDER

# SURRENDER

## Blame

> Then the man said, "The woman whom You gave to be with me, she gave me of the tree, and I ate."
>
> —Genesis 3:12

Blame is fitting to begin with, for the simple fact that it usually leads to surrender. How so? Well, we like to blame everyone around us for why we fall so short. We blame our circumstances that we are involved in, for the reason life is out of control. We blame God for creating us as we are or for placing us in uncontrollable situations. Blame is the beginning of selfish justification of oneself and one's actions. Blame can also be used as a fear blanket to protect us from being held accountable or dealing with issues that are unpleasant.

Blame is a denial of accountability that can lead our conscious and heart to deeper and darker levels of hardening. This is usually not realized, however, by the alcoholic or addict. To be honest, it is usually not realized by most of the human race. We confirm our own worst fears when accepting responsibilities for mistakes. We confirm our inability to control all things. We sink into depression when giving thought to what we view as our failures. After all, we are unworthy and not good enough. We know this, but we don't want the rest of the world discovering our secret. I was constantly angry and afraid all the world, friends, and loved ones really thought that way about me already, but I was bound and determined to prove them wrong.

Then there is another form of blame: the soul of desperation that blames itself for every single problem that arises; and the individual who only stops blaming their self when under the influence of alcohol, drugs, and any obsessive lifestyle that enables short-lived rendezvous through wiping away our consciousness. Both versions of blame are dangerous and unhealthy. Each one will lead to a boiling point where the human spirit has to be forgiven of its hypocrisy or plunge itself into selfish actions of sin to temporarily relieve the pain.

In Genesis 3:12, we see the first human created on earth using the self-denial mechanism of blame. Adam is claiming he merely ate the fruit Eve gave him. He is also blaming God for being the one to give him Eve—that is a further attempt to remove himself from responsibility of his actions. As a result, Adam and Eve are made to leave the Garden of Eden. Does blame not spiral? From the fall of Adam and Eve, all mankind has been placed in a position of having to seek God rather than walk with Him. What if Adam had said, "Lord,

I have done wrong. I was selfish and disobeyed You. Please forgive me?"

What if we had taken responsibility for our mistakes and sins long before we had reached the point of brokenness and removal from our Garden of Eden? What if we could surrender blame and the need to justify or condemn ourselves constantly, before we had reached the point of no return? Unfortunately, we are too fearful, prideful, and selfish to usually point the blame where it needs to be. The blame lies in the lack of our relationship with God and our selfish removal of His presence in our hearts.

In my last bout of alcoholism, there was a slow wave of blame that manifested into a major tsunami by the end. I was trying to be the man I always felt I needed to be. I had a very good job. I had a wonderful wife who stood by me through tough times, that was nothing short of a miracle in itself. We had four healthy children, a nice home, and financially we had come through a rough season but were looking forward to brighter days ahead. We enjoyed a loving and supportive family, and we spent time together as often as possible. We also had become members of a local church for the first time in our lives and attended almost every Sunday. There was no excuse for the events that followed to ever take place. Well, actually there was.

Once again, I began to obsess over timelines, expectations, and details that I felt needed to be met. I began attempting to control every aspect of life—the amount of money we made, how much we should have in the bank, how our children should act, the hours I spent a day in my garden and in my career, etc.

These obsessions came about very slowly and well disguised, but were there nonetheless. As I allowed myself to be more engulfed with my own righteousness, I began to blame circumstances for why expectations were not met. I also blamed others for their lack of discipline and commitment. I truly became a self-proclaimed judge of everything and everyone around me.

Then there were bouts of the other extreme when I blamed myself for not measuring up to expectations and blamed others for being created perfectly while I was a worthless lump of humanity. I finally realized that I could not control the promotion I felt I deserved at work or the fixing of my children that I thought was needed. Also, the financial situation was not at all where I felt it should be, and I believed that was due to my own foolish spending and inability to earn enough. I started to let the feelings of worthlessness and despair set in. As a result, I began to drink again in a concealed manner, and when confronted, I lied about doing it. Then of course, all the shame and guilt began to return from the past that I never felt freed from, along with the new failure and misery I was embarking upon. I began to become resentful of who I was, the people around me, and why God placed me in this position again. I truly hated myself. There was a war within myself at all times. The only mechanism available to me for peace was to drink which would start the vicious cycle all over again. I wanted peace and success. I longed for an answer. At this time in my life, there was little to no relationship with Jesus Christ. I had plenty of religion throughout my life, but no true relationship with Christ to speak of.

I was in need of a spiritual overhaul but had no foundation to build upon to take the steps needed to begin. I couldn't possibly ask for help, that would make my own convictions of worthlessness official. All I knew to do, at the time, was continue to fight by my own means and hope I would somehow fix the situation; however, I simply made matters worse. My drinking increased along with blaming everything in my life. I became thoroughly intoxicated one night and went home to my wife and kids and informed them, I was not worthy of the marriage. I thought I was setting them free to pursue happiness in life. I would merely be in their way and was no more than a worthless alcoholic. I also informed my wife, I would be pursuing another woman. You see, when I had reached my point of throwing in the towel, my blinded mind and soul only viewed my selfishness and what could be used to fulfill some sort of physical and mental relief. I was concerned for my wife and children, their future, and the shame this would cause them, but let's be honest about the situation. The number one person I was really concerned about was me! At that point in time in my thought process, alcohol was the only means to happiness because it would drown out any feelings of remorse and guilt that would haunt any sober moment. And how do we feel some sort of value and worth when we truly question if we have any? I would seek that self value based upon what others were willing to do for me and with me. I could not identify that any individual willing to boost my ego at such a time was just as lost and desolate as I! My plan was to stay under the influence alcohol and, eventually, any drug needed to control the situation of doom-and-gloom. I planned to finish out my days under the societal disguise: "Well, he was always a good guy, but the booze got the better of him." The truth was, I wasn't a good guy or person, and I knew it!

You can only imagine the shock this had been to my family. As I said, I had been hiding things and warring within myself. Blame had become my partner in sin. Blame had allowed me to place all my selfish actions on the hearts of my family. I hated myself. I blamed myself. I blamed God. Complete despair and lost hope became the anchors that held my life's foundation firmly in the pit of mental hell.

## Question Our Existence

> "Why did the knees receive me? Or why the breasts, that I should nurse?"
>
> —Job 3:12

In this verse, Job is asking why he was ever born. Job had just gone through loss of family, possessions, friends, and all status in the world that he had attained. Job was also afflicted with physical, mental, and emotional sickness and suffering. How many of us have felt the same as Job at one time or another in life?

The next morning, I awoke and realized what my drinking and selfish life had cost my family and myself. I stared at the wall in disbelief and shock. Was this the course of my life? Was all the nurturing from childhood, training from schools, and lessons in life merely ways to pass time leading up to complete moral bankruptcy? Did my mother nurse me when I was young and my father make sure I had always been fed, for me to simply become an evil monster that would be used to destroy other loved ones lives? Were my wife and children supposed to accept my betrayal and selfish addiction and go on with their lives abandoned? I couldn't believe life had led me to this new found bottom of emotional torture once again.

I saw the pain in my wife's eyes. I felt the betrayal I had caused her each time I looked at her innocent face. I saw the abandonment in my children's faces. I felt they looked upon their father with disgust, anger, and fear. I had crushed all their dreams, securities, and sense of family. I wish I had never been born. My hate for myself grew stronger by the minute. Why did God let me destroy all that was precious to me? It was bad enough to waste my own life, but why did I have to ruin my wife and children's lives as well? I sunk into the deepest depression and fear I had ever known in my life. I longed for death. I felt pain and anxiety with every breath that entered my chest. I was daydreaming about ways to vanish and never hurt anyone or myself again!

Like Job, I stood to lose my family, possessions, and all remaining positive reputation. I was also in the midst of mental and emotional distress and physically a wreck. Unlike Job, I had brought this upon myself and my family. I carried all the guilt, shame, and resentment on my own soul. I so longed for release and peace from the burden I had acquired throughout my selfish life. I longed for that release to the point of contemplating suicide. The only thing stopping me was fear of eternal life in hell.

My thoughts of suicide lasted several days. The anxiety I felt during this time was complete misery around the clock. I could not make my mind focus on anything other than my horrible addiction and actions. I went three days with no food. I could not bring myself to eat, nor had a desire to. I drank water or coffee and that was all. It was as if there was a power greater than I pressuring me to admit defeat, bow out of the human race, and end my pain and the pain of my loved ones. I later realized that there was truly a power far greater than myself that wants to convince all of us to do the same.

The human spirit can only withstand so much misery before it will break. I was at that breaking point. One afternoon, on my way home from work, I had a discussion with God that changed my life forever. I was sure my marriage was over, my children had written me off, and I was destined to be a drunk till my dying days. I did not wish that to be my destiny. I cried out to God to forgive me. I confessed my sins and selfish life. I openly told God that I was guilty of turning away from Him. I yelled out, "God, fix me or kill me!" My entire being was involved in that request. My spirit groaned for peace and forgiveness. I was willing to accept any form of correction God had in store for me. I also asked God to take care of my wife and children, no matter what His decision was for me. I said I was a child of His, the true God. I was a child of light, and not darkness. I prayed God to deliver me from the evil and temptation I had been guilty of in life. I asked God to deliver me and my family and claim us as His children. I rebuked the devil and begged God to forever drive him out of my life.

Little did I know the answer God was about to give. At this time, I was given a small mustard seed of faith. I was not sure why other than God's intervention, but there was a fraction of hope and peace I had not known. God gave me just enough faith and courage to recognize that maybe He loved me after all. I thought to myself: If God has not removed me from the face of the earth up to this point, why?

## God Loves Us

> "For whom the Lord loves He corrects, just as a father the son in whom he delights."
>
> —Proverbs 3:12

After crying out to God for His forgiveness and help, a change began to take place from within me. I truly had a revelation that God loved me. This is the first of a few revelations I was given by God that would forever change my life and the direction of it. Now to be fair, I must admit that this change, however positive, was very small at that time. But don't miss the main point; it was a change and a change for the positive! I felt a sense of peace. I felt that I was loved—that love was coming through my spirit from God; and I did not understand it at that time, but I wanted to know more about this hope and comfort I was sensing.

This new feeling I was experiencing was not my normal outlook on God previously. I had always viewed God as this wise, judgmental, white-bearded power that sat upon a throne in the clouds looking down upon creation, shaking His head at our lack of religion. I believed God to be so unreachable that I could hardly imagine His dissatisfaction in my life and what I had chosen to do with it. I knew Jesus was the Son of God, He came to Earth, died, and rose again on the third day. I also believed that whatever it was that Jesus had done for me, I was not worthy of. I believed I was too damaged to have a close relationship with God, let alone be counted worthy of forgiveness. I felt ashamed of who I was, what I had done, and nowhere close to measuring up to God's expectations of me.

Why wouldn't I have this outlook on God? After all, I had lived all my life feeling unlovable, unwanted, unworthy, and not equal to others. My experiences with God had been one religious expectation after another of God's awesome power that left me under the impression I was a disappointment. I mean, God had done so much for me, yet I did not return the respect and discipline needed to be counted worthy. My desires of God were portrayed through rituals of man and a sacrifice of time once per week at church.

I did not recognize that my heart was longing for so much more interaction with God. I did not even know that the hole in my soul that I had been trying to fill all my life was the absence of my relationship with God.

How often has this world and man-made traditions stood between ourselves and the furthering of our relationship with God? So many of us are told to make a particular sacrifice that we do not understand. We are told to commit our lives to God at a certain age when we are in no way able to perform the commitment we are making. We are brought up in a repetitive, routine, and stagnant religion. Now there is no rule that says religion has to be exciting and fun all the time, but isn't our eternal soul worth putting some sense of emotion toward? Don't worry, I'm not resorting to blame again. I am merely stating the reason why my religious beliefs never led me to a relationship with God other than unworthiness is because I sought religion and not God. I looked at man's traditions and expectations on religious beliefs. I did not look at God's heart and desire for intimacy with me through His word.

That's where I came to understand that through the prayer I cried out in voice and spirit that day in my truck, God responded directly to me out of love. At this time, I began to read the Bible on my own for the first time in my life in an attempt to confirm that feeling I had received. God answered me through the pages that I read. I went right to the New Testament and started with the Gospel of Matthew. I began to see time and time again the love God has for us. John 3:16 is the greatest verse contained in the Bible to prove this love:

> For God so loved the world that He gave His only begotten Son, that whoever believes in Him should not perish but have everlasting life.

Proverbs 3:12 tells us that God does indeed love us. Not only as a God-to-creation relationship but as a father-to-son relationship. We see that God delights in our correction through Him. Correction in the sense of a father-and-son relationship is based upon love and hope that the son will grow, strengthen, and know the fullness of life. This is exactly what God wants for each one of us. God delights in our correction, because it will lead us directly to Him in a more intimate relationship. God has our attention when we are truly broken. When we reach the point of desperation and lost hope for anything joyful, we are open to suggestions and advice. How often did we accept advice before we reached our sense of doom? From my own experience, I can honestly say I seldom listened to any advice while in my selfish life of addiction and chaos.

If God truly loves us as a father loves a son, then that makes us His child. Would a loving father ever abandon his child? Would a loving father not give his child the correction, support, and tools needed to help him succeed and right the wrongs he has done? At times our Father may let us travel head first into the brick wall we are bound and determined to crash into, in order to let us come to that place of surrender. Once we finally impact, however, who is the first one to help us back up? Who is it that gives us the courage to try again? Who is it that tells us what we need to change and what we need to build upon? It is always our loving Father!

That loving Father just so happens to be the creator of the universe and all contained therein. God is our loving Father and He loves each and every one of us with a passion and pureness we can only imagine. When we first ask God into our lives and confess our sins, God's spirit sings for joy. There is singing and praising in heaven from the angels and there is rejoicing throughout (Luke 15:7, 10). The parable of the prodigal son (Luke 15:11–32) best explains the relationship our heavenly Father longs to have with us. If God did not love us with such passion, why would the enemy of God, Satan, be so determined to steal our soul away from Him? The human soul is precious and extremely valuable to God. When we begin to surrender our life to God, we will feel some peace and relief from the anguish we have known. This peace is our spirit desperately reaching out to the spirit of God and receiving a response, begging for forgiveness, longing for comfort, and clinging to a shred of hope that God can and will correct us.

When I first felt the presence and love of God, it was as if my inner spirit had received the thirst-quenching drink it had so longed for. My eyes watered up with tears of joy. I felt a weight fall from my soul and there was a sense that everything would be okay. I actually felt as though I was in the loving protection of my God, and He would keep me safe when the world only left me desolate. I ceased my personal torture of myself and thanked God for life. God was beginning the transformation of His child whom He loved. The courts of heaven rejoiced with angelic harmony.

God does love you. The Bible tells us again and again of His love for us. No matter what you have done in life and how far away you have drifted from God, He will forgive you. God will correct you, redeem you, and give you joy. Be patient and enjoy this new found love God has shown you. With the feeling of true love and purposeful correction from God, we can begin to see more clearly His wisdom and path in which we are to walk. Dedicate your heart and soul to God and His word. Give as much time as possible to the Bible, and watch the writings of God come to life in your spirit.

## God Knows What Is Best

> "I know that nothing is better for them than to rejoice, and to do good in their lives."
>
> —Ecclesiastes 3:12

Once we discover and feel the love God has for us, we begin to almost unconsciously rejoice. Our mood and demeanor seems a bit more stable and we lose some of the me, me, and me attitude. We can see outside of ourselves for the first time in awhile and focus on God and loved ones and attempting to serve them. This is a radical change of heart for the individual who has been lost in their own selfishness through addictions and sin. Is this by our own resources or intelligence you may ask? Not at all. God knows exactly what is needed to begin molding His child into the loving, obedient servant He has chosen us to be.

Ecclesiastes 3:12 tells us to rejoice and do good. It goes as far as telling us nothing is better for us than rejoicing and doing good! That is quite a statement God wants us to hear. Why the strong emphasis on these two actions? Well, we are coming out of a life of personal and worldly condemnation. Circumstances that have given us little reason to collect a positive thought at all, let alone rejoice. Circumstances such as years of substance abuse, depression, divorce, prison, loss of job, attempted suicide, family abandonment, loss of loved ones and the list goes on and on. We have been an ocean of doubts and disappointments. Our mind and spirit have been the main chains of bondage, restraining us from any kind of happiness. Our deeds and actions have been a direct result of what our mind had been: negative and ungodly. God wants us to start seeing our lives and His presence with us in a completely different light. We need to begin to let God transform our minds and spirit into the creation He made us to be.

This begins with the ability to identify the blessings God has bestowed upon us and share those blessings with others. God has given us so much to be thankful for. Most of us have some sort of family, support, or loved ones who never turned their back on us when times get tough. We have our beautiful world God has created and given for our lives and enjoyment. We all eat food each and every day, have the air that we breathe, and have God's holy words to give us courage. Most of all, we have the love of our creator who longs to have a personal relationship with us. We are at a stage where we can truly recognize and appreciate the little things in life. As we further read the Bible and uncover God's word, we see the overwhelming evidence that God wants us joyful and happy not only in heaven with Him one day, but in this present life as well. As we begin to become more positive and thankful, we find our new mentality taking over as opposed to our negative thought process that brought us to our demise. A thankful attitude leads to giving and helping.

We are so accustomed to feeling sorry for ourselves. We have always dwelled upon how much better everyone else's life was than ours. We complain about our circumstances, how misfortunate the world has treated us, and our inability to get a break like everyone else. We selfishly sought to further fill our worldly desires without being thankful to what we had been given. At times we are the perfect example of a three-year-old child in a grocery store, throwing a fit over not getting what we grabbed onto from out of the cart. How would anyone give an ounce of energy to help another with the mindset we had been trapped in? It was all about us, for us, and owed to us! We have to get some humility and joy into our minds that will slowly begin chasing out the selfish corruption of sin we have dwelt in.

Here's a couple of very important points that need to be discussed at this time.

1. It is crucial to get plugged into a loving church family.
2. Don't let the enemy steal your joy.

My wife and I made the commitment to serve God as best we could. We surrendered our lives and asked God to guide us by His spirit and fill us with joy and peace. In return, God brought us into a true church family. A church family is not the same as a building where like-minded members of the same denomination meet once a week for their obligated time to the Lord. We entered a set of doors where the people inside welcomed us immediately with open arms. They hugged us, shook our hands, asked us our reason for being there, and we were invited to dinner by three different couples that first day. Those couples are still inviting us to dinner and are as sincere today as they were the first day we met. Through those acquaintances we have found true friends that will encourage, pray, hold us accountable, and discuss all things pertaining to our lives individually and as a couple. Most importantly, they taught us how to truly rejoice!

Our pastor and his wife encouraged us to get involved and help those less fortunate. They took the time to counsel us and grow us in Christ. Above all, they taught us to rejoice. God will put us in contact with those who will strengthen us in His name. Spend the time and go church shopping. Find the church that truly is an example of a family. One that will share your hopes and dreams, and always listen to your fears and concerns. Also, find one that is willing to put you to work for the good of the whole church family. It is important to feel we are giving back some of the joy God has blessed us with.

Beware of the enemy. If you think for one single minute Satan will sit back and admit defeat, you are seriously wrong. You are beginning to sense God's spirit and peace. You are rejoicing in what God has given you and wishing to perform good works for God and others. You are no longer a sideliner in the kingdom of God, you are becoming a player. Satan will come after you with new trials and old memories. Satan attempted to sway Jesus Christ Himself from His mission (Matt 4:1-11, Luke 4:1-13). Do you think he won't come after you? Satan hates you. He wants to separate you from God again. That is what we were before surrendering our life to God—separated. Expect any and every little thing at times that can go wrong to go wrong. Expect bouts of negative thoughts where we try to slip into our past and doubt that we can continue on this new journey. Do not be moved when others doubt us and try to condemn us again of past mistakes. God has forgiven us for all our transgressions, don't let Satan deceive us into thinking we're not forgiven.

What do we choose to be consumed by? We will be an image and reflection of what we choose to let consume us. If we choose to be consumed by selfishness, fear, doubt, worry, greed, lust, addictions, etc, we will be the reflection of that person who is led by such actions. If we are consumed by the perceptions of who we think we are to be and who the world says we need to be, we will reflect a worldly man consumed by our self righteousness and anxiety to live up to those expectations. We will be the image of one all alone to face the world.

That being said, if we choose to be consumed by the promises of Jesus Christ, what will happen? If we choose to be consumed with joy of salvation in Christ, forgiveness and grace from God, and obedient with the teachings of God's word....will we not reflect and imagine a person who is joyous in their salvation, forgiven and forgiving, and anxious to spread their salvation and good news to others whom also may want salvation? The image of one confident they will never be forsaken, forgotten, or orphaned!

Our thoughts are our own choice. We can listen to God's spirit, which bestows peace and love, or we can be prisoners to the attacks of the enemy that are doubt and fear. A key scripture to remember and use as defense when the negative thoughts try to enter our mind is from 2 Timothy 1:7,

> For God has not given us a spirit of fear, but of power and of love and of sound mind.

We will be far from perfect with our rejoicing. We have suffered with addictions and suffered our lives with sin. We longed for a quick and immediate fix to the problems we could not overcome. God has given us forgiveness and enabled us to feel some joy and peace. We are still human, however, and will at times fight ourselves. We must not give up, give in, or give out along this journey. Remember, God will correct us. We will long for complete healing immediately. Some healing takes longer and has a greater purpose for God's glory when accomplished. God loves us; He wants us joyful and doing good in our life. We can do this if we stay surrendered. There were times in my early walk with the Lord that I did not feel like rejoicing in the least bit. I wanted to slip back into my chamber of despair and self-pity. God gave me the wisdom to identify this for what it was; my selfishness and doubts and my concerns about me and not my focus on others. God gave me the strength at times to thank Him, rejoice, and be hopeful even when that was not at all my mood. Through this attitude, a pattern is established that will make it harder and harder to return to our old way of thinking.

We may suffer during this stage of our transformation. God doesn't say this is easy, but He does say His grace is sufficient. Rejoice in the Lord always and give thanks for His blessings. Praise God with all your soul and long to feel more and more of His presence. Pray and talk with God constantly and give no open door for the devil to enter. We have spent our entire life trying to live it our way; how did that work? Give an open mind and heart to God and truly take the words from Ecclesiastes 3:12 to heart. Serve others, rejoice in God's love, and let things fall into place. In time, this will shine light on the real issues that caused us to stray from our God to begin with.

## The World Leads to Death

> As for my people, children are their oppressors, and women rule over them. O My people! Those who lead you cause you to err, and destroy the way of your paths.
>
> —Isaiah 3:12

After some time of praising God and doing good with our lives, at least as good as we can, we start to feel conviction against the way we had lived before. It will become more and more apparent that our lives were based on the perceptions of our minds and how it was supposed to be, rather than on God's word. We can see we pursued happiness in all the wrong places and through all the wrong methods. We chased after our dreams and goals that usually amounted into selfish desires and wants. We begin to see clearly for the first time in our lives. We were truly blinded, but now begin to see! We were lost, but now through God's mercy, we are found. What we will usually identify at this time is just how wrong and misled we have been.

That is exactly what God is telling us in Isaiah 3:12. He is pointing out where our lives that led us to complete destruction began. Somewhere along the way we fell victim to identity theft in this world. We lost our true identity as a child of God and became *gods* in our own mind. Even those of us who felt inadequate and worthless are guilty of a perception of our own divinity. There are a few different ways of accomplishing the same dreadful results of identity theft. We would have to be nearly perfect to escape this snare that so many of us fall victim to, and as a result become in bondage to our own self shackled chains.

I will use myself as an example of this thievery that steers so many astray from our true course in life. I was always a fairly-good child growing up. I had a normal childhood and was a member of a comfortable middle class family. My mother watched over her children very closely, and my father was a hardworking man. Sure they had some arguments at times, but there was a definite sense of security in our home.

I looked upon my father as no mere mortal. He was tall, strong, wise, and always seemed in control of every situation in which life placed him. If ever I had done wrong and tried to pull the wool over my father's eyes, he knew it immediately. Somewhere along the way, at an early age, and to the best of my recollection, I began to feel I could never be the man my father was. There was no good excuse for this. My father never belittled me or made me feel anything other than supported. Sure he was disappointed a few times, but I never felt as if his love for me was any less. Where did such a notion come from in my mind? My father, while he was alive, was my best friend and biggest fan and I knew this. Something made me feel inadequate.

My mother was another example of this. She would fight to death for any one of her children on the drop of a hat. She was a wonderful mother and always put her children first. Make no mistake, she let me know when she was displeased, but never did I feel anything less than loved by my mother. Then I began to notice my attitude around other kids my age and people in general. I never felt like I was on quite the same level. I always saw others as people who had it all together and were perfect. I was like a fish out of water around a crowd. In sports, I was a nervous wreck and suffered self inflicted anxiety before sporting events. My biggest fear was I would lose the game for the team, and they would discover just how big of an underachiever I really was. I ended up getting a scholarship in football, and remember how much I dreaded the thought of my misery continuing another four years. Now, I had the whole town I grew up in watching to see me fall, and if I did, then the truth would finally be out. I wasn't any good to begin with. My drinking took care of the scholarship. I was flunking out and in trouble shortly into the first year, and therefore, left with my tail tucked between my legs. Freedom at last!

Some freedom that was. The point is that at the time, it truly did feel like freedom. Some of the pressure and expectations I had mounted upon my shoulders was relieved at the time. I lost my true identity early on when I began setting expectations for myself and not heeding what God had in plan for me. I placed what I felt was a powerful successful man in front of anything God had to say on the issue. I also strived to control and fix any and all circumstances. I was trying to keep the perception going that I had it all together and needed no help. I would never even dream of asking for help. What an embarrassment that would have been! I made myself out to be the complete and total power in my world and the world of others. I tried to manage and conquer all things alone and never cried uncle. I placed myself in the position where God was supposed to have and I did not have a clue I had done it. After all, any man worth his salt could handle any and all crisis on his own, right?

We are part of a society that tells us to make this much money per year to be successful. We are told to drive this kind of car; after all you don't want the neighbor having one before you. Wear these designer clothes, buy this type of food, give this answer to your critics, etc. The list goes on and on. We are pressured at early ages from peers and society to engage in sex, alcohol, drugs, and rebellious behavior just to be recognized as cool. The thought of being deemed a goody two shoes or choir boy in today's culture is absolutely terrifying and sure to cause excommunication from the "in crowd." Adults suffer from the same anxiety of unpopularity just as our youth do. We trample our brothers and sisters under our feet in order to fill our lustful greed, pride, and selfishness. Our children idolize every major self-absorbed sport jockey there is. We feel we are good parents if we buy our children the most expensive pair of shoes, or put on the biggest birthday party in town for them.

Too often our money and possessions are taking the place of advice and conversation that our children really could benefit from. We roll red carpets out for movie stars that have a different husband or wife every eighteen months—and those are the devoted ones. We watch television programs with one example after another of no morals or values, and demeaning images that stick like glue in our minds. We place all our resources, time, and abilities in pursuing what the world has told us are important. Material things and ball games on Sunday have surpassed the Bible and church.

We set ourselves prisoners in our own minds of greed and selfishness. We not only feel the need to keep up with society, a lot of us feel we have to be the overwhelming conqueror of society to reach happiness.

We chase the American dream, but maybe the dream isn't worth chasing any longer. If the dreams and pleasures of this world lead us into the damnation and torture of our eternal life, what good is it?

The world will have us chasing our identity, or should I say what we think our current identity in the world needs to be, every single minute of the day. It is easy to get lost and become completely hopeless on the path the world guides us upon. It is a broad and wide path which leads to death!

You have heard me mention the enemy a few times already in previous chapters. Let me bring him into the conversation again. Satan, the enemy, pretty well runs things down here on earth. Satan was cast out of heaven for the following reasons: pride, ego, selfishness, and greed. He wanted to be like God and above God Himself. Sound familiar? The majority of the world suffers from these same issues. At times, they may manifest their self in another form. These are harder to identify but feed off the same principals—fear, doubt, worthlessness, and despair. How do these very different problems people suffer relate?

Fear can be the same as pride in opposite fashion. When we are fearful we are saying I do not want to be exposed or revealed as opposed to being the main object of attention. There may be something I don't like or others may exploit.

Doubt is a lack of our ego and longing for more.

Worthlessness is feeling opposite of selfishness. Or is it? We say we're not good enough and don't deserve anything but groaning for attention and comfort. We are actually saying to everyone who listens, to please focus on us feeling better.

Finally, despair is feeling like we have less and less of what we need and long for. That is a disguised version of greed.

Satan will get to know us and realize if we are strong or weak in all these areas. Then, he will fuel the fire once he sees an imbalance that can be used to destroy the human most soundly. Sometimes he will fuel several different fires within us at once, making us completely in bondage to the world and hopeless at the time. He will not give us a chance to catch our breath. The flames will consume us and burn till all remnants of God are disposed of from within the human heart.

The world truly does lead to death. We will not overcome it by our own resources. We need to look at who we were, and what God has delivered us from. The human alone cannot overcome Satan when we are subjected to the world and give into its identity theft. The one and only hope is in God. When we realize our past mistakes and just how wicked and deceitful the world and our enemy can be, we should give praise and thanks to our Father each and every day for delivering us from the evil we knew. God has taken us off the broad path and is setting us on a new journey where the path is narrow and straight…straight to His Kingdom! During this process we will see many things about ourselves of which we will not approve. Remember, God has forgiven us and loves us. Do not get caught up in guilt and shame that our Heavenly Father has set us free of! Satan will be lying in wait to penetrate any crack in the fortress of God we are building upon within our minds and soul. Rejoice and do good! Infection cannot set into the body that has the remedy in its veins. God's word is the remedy.

## Surrender to God's Will and Holy Spirit

> Then the Spirit lifted me up, and I heard behind me a great thunderous voice: Blessed is the glory of the Lord from His place!
>
> —Ezekiel 3:12

All the previous chapters to this point have placed the emphasis on surrender. We have two more chapters and verses to look into in the phase of surrender as formatted in 3:12 Transformation. This particular chapter and verse is the one that truly enabled any chains of bondage that remained. It could hinder further growth to shatter with an understanding of truth never before felt in my soul! In "God Loves Us (Proverbs 3:12)," I spoke of a revelation when first feeling and believing God's love for me. I will explain in this chapter another revelation that completely altered my direction in life and placed my journey in the hands of the Lord.

I had begun seeking counseling and guidance from a pastor at a church not too far from where I lived. Although this was a local church, it was far from any previous church atmosphere I had ever known. People seemed happy to be there and not at all rushed to get to their cars as soon as the service ended. It was as if they enjoyed themselves and enjoyed each other's company. I had been used to attending church where people did not communicate with each other outside a simple hello, goodbye, or how's work? Also, I always felt like the entire church was staring at me in judgment of my past or present distress with alcoholism or my marriage. But this church felt different. I felt welcomed and accepted. I remember thinking to myself, *This is odd; these people act as if they like the fact that I am here and not like I am offending them by showing my face in church.* I tried to convince my wife to attend with me, but at the time she was still not quite sold on my new found optimism. She was not sold on me at the time yet either to be perfectly honest. The pastor met with both of us individually and asked our history; events that brought us where we were and where we wished to go from that point. He suggested marriage counseling and spending as much time with fellow Christians as possible. Like I said already, my wife was not sold on all that just yet. I, however, being the reason again for any hardships between my wife and I, was very cooperative and eager to take the pastor's advice. I began meeting with the pastor once per week, attending church to hear him every Sunday, and fellowshipping with a few of the church members who gave wonderful support and encouragement to me when needed most.

The pastor recommended I undergo a new believer's study course with him. I have to admit, I felt a little above the new believers stuff. After all, I had been raised in a church most of my life. I had performed all the required sacraments and requirements and believed in God and Jesus. But I figured God had a reason for the course, and if I truly desired to change my life it was best to be open-minded and willing. I began to study the booklet he had given me for the course, fill out the questions at the end of each weekly assignment, and discuss the assignment with him each week when we would meet. This gave me more and more opportunity to read, study, research the Bible, and dive deeper into topics of faith I had not looked into before. I knew a lot of the Bible stories from childhood and many names of the stories; however, I began to see the readings meant much more at this time. The Bible was speaking directly to me, my circumstances, and my feelings. It was every bit as relevant to me in this day and age as it was when it was written a few thousand years ago. I was feeling optimistic and encouraged at the direction my life was heading. I had moved on past blaming myself, surroundings, God, and others for every negative memory of the past with honest accountability and remorse for my actions. I was no longer wishing for death and questioning why I had ever been born. I felt the love, forgiveness, and presence of God for the first time in my life. I was learning through God's word and other Christians to rejoice and do good deeds for others. I looked at my past wickedness and doubts, fears and failures, disappointments and betrayals, and honestly recognized the error of my selfish ways. What was missing? Why did I not stumble onto this new life in God long before? Why was I unable to control my recovery and surrender up to that point?

This is exactly the question I asked the pastor one afternoon: Why could I not come to this understanding and surrender before pastor? Why did I try so hard to control things with the best of intentions at the start, only to fail time and time again? Then the pastor responded a simple but profound statement I will never forget: "If you could have overcome these things on your own, why did Jesus Christ hang upon the cross?" I can only explain with words that will not do justice to the feeling I had at that moment. My eyes were opened! My ears finally truly heard! I understood! I sensed a feeling of warmth, and tingles run through my body. I felt a releasing of weight and surrendering of questions. I felt an approval from the Lord our God as if He was saying, "You finally hear the truth I have tried to show you!" Whatever weight of shame, guilt, and despair was still hanging upon me was dropped at that very instant in time. Oh, how I had missed who Jesus Christ was and what He had done!

My eyes were filled with tears of joy and acceptance of forgiveness and salvation. Jesus truly had paid my penalty. That is why He hung on the cross. Christ knew I would fall short of the glory of God. Christ knew I would battle the world and the lusts contained in it and on my own power would lose the battle in epic proportion. Jesus took the beatings, so I could be forgiven of my wrongs. Christ took the scourging, so I could avoid punishment of hell. Jesus was crucified and died upon the cross to give me a hope of life. Our Lord, Jesus Christ rose from the dead to give me victory over sin and the death I knew in this world and provide everlasting life with the Father in Heaven. Jesus did this for me! Jesus did this for all of us! I never saw Jesus Christ as my one and only personal savior before that day. Then I remembered that the Father and the Son are one and realized that Jesus Christ, my God, died for us because of His great unquenchable, burning love He has for us all. How much He must love us!

I left the meeting that day with a new outlook on everything in life. Forgiveness of oneself and belief in forgiveness from our God is an overwhelming emotion of hope and power that turns into faith and peace. Now, I truly started experiencing peace—peace that I had never known or thought possible. How can the brutal death of a man who was nailed to a cross, ridiculed, and scorned give a person such peace? Through His sacrifice of love, He gave His life as ransom for all our sins. All we have done against God that we could never make right by our own works were erased the instant we accept Jesus Christ's sacrifice for us, and ask Him into our heart. This is the moment when we hear the truth, and accept it for what I believe truth is… God's Grace!

> Because of the hope which is laid up for you in heaven, of which you heard before in the word of the truth of the gospel, which has come to you, as it has also in all the world, and is bringing forth fruit, as it is also among you since the day you heard and knew the grace of God in truth.
>
> Colossians 1:5,6

The deepest fear of our soul is what happens after death. Jesus Christ removes that fear when we ask Him into our heart and seek His example in our everyday life. The fear turns into faith of who we are and where we are going. We are children of God—beloved and precious; we are children who will spend eternity with their loving Father in heaven. Regardless of our past, Christ gave us forgiveness and future. My spirit was filled with new found hope, optimism, conviction, and longing to follow the example Jesus had set for us.

God's Holy Spirit was lifting me up to a new height and giving me understanding and insight on His power, glory, and love through Jesus Christ. I even remember feeling lighter when I walked out of the church that day. God gave me a surge of faith that has stayed upon me and increased over time. True worship and praise began flowing out of my lips more readily, and the awesomeness of God was true to me as never before. The burden I felt was released from the guilt I could never let go of before. How could of I? I believed by my own power I could eventually make things right, be the man I was supposed to be, and overcome alcoholism and the world. I failed every time and always made issues worse and more desperate. The burden of guilt and failure grew heavier with each failed attempt. Jesus Christ hung each of our bags of burdens upon the cross in the form of His flesh. Why should any of us carry the burden Christ has taken away from us any longer?

If we choose not to accept Christ's sacrifice like we have done so many times before, we are telling God thanks for the thought, but no thanks. If we once again take the selfish attitude that we can handle things on our own and keep God at a safe arms length away, we are removing our burdens from the cross and carrying them again. Jesus Christ died for this freedom that we can share and feel. Why should we any longer mock the ultimate sacrifice He made for us, and threaten our eternity separated from Him? As humans, we cannot imagine God's wisdom and sovereign power. In this wisdom, He has chosen the sacrifice of His Son as our atonement for sin. I plead with you all to make the decision in your heart to accept this sacrifice presented to us from God, our Father Himself, and cease your disbelief in the cross of Christ any longer. Through the cross we are set free, and all things in time will be revealed to us.

God's power is awesome and great! God's mercies and forgiveness are bountiful and abundant. God's love is greater than all! We will all have different testimonies of true surrender. I am blessed to share mine with you. I do want to express that through this stage of our surrender and transformation we are further prepared for God's will for each one of us individually. We are increasingly accessible for God's Holy Spirit to fill us. As we see in Ezekiel 3:12, there will come a time during our surrender that God will lift us up to a higher level of truth and spiritual awareness. Our stories will differ, but I believe we will all have a distinct personal experience during our surrender. The moment we realize God's Holy Spirit is lifting us up and taking us where we could never go alone. Our path and purpose becomes clearer and will be pointed in one main direction and toward one man in particular! Jesus Christ is the way, the truth, and the life.

## Humility and Peace: Trust in the Lord

> I will leave in your midst a meek and humble people and they shall trust in the name of the Lord.
>
> —Zephaniah 3:12

*Surrender*! The same word I heard all my life; the same word I frequently tried to master by my own will so many times. The mere word itself is just a series of letters formed into a three syllable sound that explains an event in one's life or a decision of one's life. But I realized surrender was so much more than a word or temporary decision. Surrender was an action that, if truly brought forth from sincerity, would control one's journey for the remainder of their lives. This action required a releasing of things that I never felt necessary before. Letting go of things, which I once believed to be positive traits that were merely negative attributes disguised as values. I was completely wrong on my viewpoint of surrender in previous years. I felt my surrender would relate to a happy family and an ability to control things without causing damage. I believed it would supply wisdom and peace in this world from my own resources and accomplishments. That was surrender to me—the ability to avoid a future failure because of my will power to control the events in my life. I felt the issues needed to be surrendered in earlier years were alcohol and my weak will power. If I could get past those two glaring downfalls, all else would fall into place and life would be smooth. I really believed one could strengthen their will power, as if building muscles of the body, by one's own means.

What a fool I had been! Surrender was not at all what my perception had made it out to be. I remember feeling this shortly after accepting Jesus Christ as my personal savior and Lord; however, the funny thing was, I was not ashamed of the fact that I had been wrong for so many years. To be honest, I was relieved. I knew from that moment on that my failures and disappointments and the ability to fix them were beyond my control and anyone else's without Jesus Christ. Therefore, a new form of surrender had been and was taking place in my life. What truly needed surrendered that had not been in previous years? What truly needed embraced that was neglected in prior attempts? We must surrender our resentment toward others and our resentment toward ourselves. We must let go of our past shame and guilt.

We must cast aside our previous forms of healing and become open to the healing of God.

Surrender the false identity the world has implanted into our minds since we can remember. Do not fall again into continued dwelling of the past. Look ahead in hopes of the goodness and promises to come. Surrender our selfishness and attempts to control our very surrender. We have failed and will fail by our own power! Surrender your every ounce of being to Jesus Christ and His teachings. Jesus surrendered all for each one of us. He set the example of surrender. Give willingly and openly of oneself. Be a servant and a kind soul to all those we know whether they are family, friends, or strangers. Be obedient to God's word and will for us even if led to death in order to accomplish that will! If one is truly honest, then we will see that is where our surrender in Christ leads us. Death to the selfish world we have known—death from sin and death from wickedness and new life in God through Jesus Christ.

During this transformation, we are given the faith and strength to identify, confess, and embrace this wisdom God is showing us. I began to look at myself in very different eyes than ever before. I had a sense of humility I never before experienced—not humility in the sense of shame in any means. I humbly confessed my failures and sins in front of fellow brothers and sisters, with the confidence I was forgiven by God for all of them. I was humbled at the fact God loved me to the point of condemning His Son to death that I may have salvation. I knew my place. I was not an all powerful human that needed to prove to everyone that no matter what I had been through, I was still standing due to my special abilities to fix things. I was simply a man who was shown grace and love through God our Father. I was given forgiveness for my transgressions because of Jesus Christ alone. Nothing I had done was responsible for my transformation other than asking God for forgiveness and accepting Jesus Christ into my heart. My only part to play was true surrender—as true as humanly possible. I need to surrender each and every day to my Lord and that will never change. Unfortunately, at times my surrender is still too late, and I say things I regret, but they are quickly identified and resolved with humility and ownership. I am not perfect and neither will you ever be. I do trust, however, that continued growth in Christ will bring us closer and closer to perfection and eternity with our Father in heaven!

Surrender! Surrender is trust, willingness to be led, taught, provided for, and if need be corrected by beliefs in our lives. That is what surrender means to me today. Zephaniah 3:12 tells us that God will leave in, the midst of His people, meekness, humility, and trust in the name of the Lord. I made a choice that I press toward each and every day in life to surrender my life to God and His Son, Jesus Christ. I fall short some days and you will too. But surrender is a lifelong process and not an overnight process. For our lifelong journey, there are certain things we need to do. Study the word of God. Fill our minds with Jesus Christ's example of surrender, again and again. Place our time and resources in trusting God and His plan for us. Become a servant and blessing to others around us. Our prayer life needs constant attention. We need to let God hear from us as much as possible and be open to hear from Him. We must stay surrendered and realize that Jesus Christ died on the cross to forgive us of our sins, relieve us of past hurts, and bestow within us happiness, joy, and hope of a new life in Him. I am willing to follow a man who loved me to the point of giving His life for my well-being! I am willing to lay all my prayers and dreams before the throne of God and ask His guidance and wisdom. If God spared not His Son for us, why would He spare His guidance and wisdom if we ask? Trust in the Lord our God and stay humble in His presence and thankful in His ears!

At times, we will want to pull back our surrender for our own defense, righteousness, and selfishness. I would wager that Jesus wanted to avoid the cross and anguish as a human and not bear the humility it caused Him to suffer. What gave Him the ability to stay so surrendered to God's will? I believe it could have only been His undying faith and trust in the Father. What an example Jesus set for us! He had the ability to crush the crowds of people and all involved with His wrongful persecution; yet He followed the will of the Father and remained surrendered. Christ remained meek, humble, and obedient in the Father. Our savior not only gave us eternal salvation and life but the greatest example of trust and humility we could ever learn from.

## SURRENDER

*3:12 Transformation*

Have you used blame throughout your life? (Blamed circumstances, others, yourself, God)

___

___

___

___

Has there ever been a time in your life when you questioned your very existence?

Do you believe that God truly loves you? Are you willing to accept His love, guidance and correction in your life?

How do you plan to defend your mind against negative thoughts and pessimism?

Have your views of success in this world changed?

Do you believe God's Holy Spirit will guide and strengthen you? Do you have an experience where you believe this has happened?

______________________________________________

______________________________________________

______________________________________________

______________________________________________

Explain what you feel God asks of us in surrendering to Him.

______________________________________________

______________________________________________

______________________________________________

______________________________________________

BELIEVE
SURRENDER

# BELIEVE

## God Is Merciful

> Go and proclaim these words toward the north, and say: Return, backsliding Israel, says the Lord; I will not cause My anger to fall on you. For I am merciful, says the Lord; I will not remain angry forever.
>
> —Jeremiah 3:12

We have reached the point of surrender—true surrender for the first time in our lives. A few questions at this time: will we stay surrendered to something we cannot believe in? Will we stay surrendered to something we believe will not have mercy upon us? Will we stay surrendered to something that will remain angry with us forever? We might for awhile, but it will not last. God tells us to believe His anger will not last forever and that He will be merciful. He does stress that we need to be responsible for our sins and confess them. He tells us to return to Him and acknowledge with a broken and contrite heart that we turned away from Him to begin with (Jeremiah 3:13).

We may have some legal responsibilities or relational consequences through our sinful life that we need to deal with. But we must believe God is satisfied with a repenting heart and will lead us in His loving care as long as we take the responsibilities for our previous actions. King David speaks these words of God in the Psalms: "The sacrifices of God are a broken spirit, a broken and contrite heart-these, O God, You will not despise" (Psalm 51:17). God's spirit will guide us along the way and supply peace and confidence that we never knew before when coping with our penalties to society, employers, or loved ones. It really falls back to Proverbs 3:12 at this point. God does love us and will correct us! We may have some situations left to deal with, but if we are truly surrendered to God, He will lesson many of the consequences for us!

God is powerful, divine, and all knowing. We must not return to a pity party at this point in our transformation, due to circumstances we have brought upon ourselves. We truly must believe it is all part of God's correction for us. God has promised us an open door to return through. If we lose sight of the hallway of God's plan for us that extends beyond that door, we'll step back out and jeopardize our surrender. Believe that we will be recipients of mercy, grace, and above all, God's love!

How many times had we surrendered to someone that kept throwing all our past mistakes in our faces each time we showed the slightest sign of trouble?

Employers that go into defense mode as soon as any perception of repeated circumstances arise? How often have we been stereotyped as a horrible spouse, awful child, terrible person and all-around loser by the world regardless of our best efforts to do things right and with no evidence we have faltered in any way? Surrender usually constitutes a time of having to work our way out of the doghouse and regain confidence in others' eyes. With God, we are out of the doghouse immediately, once our earnest request of forgiveness and repentance is offered to Him. God wants us to believe now that we are forgiven and He will be merciful to us currently and in days to come. There is no need to regain God's love and mercy. It has always been there and always will be.

In Jeremiah 3:14-15, God again tells us to return to Him. He calls us His children whom He is married to and He will lead us back to Zion (Eastern hill of Jerusalem/ Where Jesus and His followers will stand in triumph on His second coming; Rev.14:1). God tells us He will give us shepherds according to His heart which will mentor, lead, and guide us along our transformations. In ministry, I have come across several men and women who claim they once have walked with God but fell away from Him. Their question is always the same: "I have backslid so far. Can God truly forgive me again? Can I feel His presence again?" My response to them is also always the same: "God has answered that question! Ask God if He forgives you, that you have walked away, and you wish to come back home to Him. Read Jeremiah 3:12-15 and tell me what God says to you!"

Time and time again throughout the Bible, God tells us of His mercy and forgiveness. Even when we have knowingly walked away from God so many times, He still will take us back and claim us as His children. We cannot go any further in our transformation with God until we truly believe we receive that forgiveness and mercy. Satan does not want to see any of us believing in this liberty and freedom God has given us. Satan prefers to see us doubtful and remorseful: imprisoned within our minds and nowhere close to feeling liberated and free.

God will not do what the rest of the world will do. God merely asks for our return to Him and confession of how we left Him to begin with. His mercy is ours from that point on. Believe we are given the mercy, no matter what life has in store for us currently or in the days to come. We have been reconciled to God through Jesus Christ! If our heart has truly surrendered to God's will then we have a new slate. Believe we are forgiven, not merely given a furlough!

## God Has the Answer

> Then the tax collectors also came to be baptized, and said to him, "Teacher, what shall we do?"
>
> —Luke 3:12

John the Baptist, was sent before Jesus Christ to pave the way for the kingdom of God! God used John to be His messenger and point the people in the direction of correction. The direction was repentance and change from within. This verse speaks of tax collectors in the time of John and Jesus. Tax collectors were considered as untrusting, immoral, and lowly people in the Jewish society, not only by their fellow brethren but also by the Romans who occupied the country. These were the people willing to sell their fellow countrymen out for profit, usury, and personal gain. The true meaning of a traitor and dishonest person were the tax collectors of that time. Sound anything like the majority of society today? These people were willing to do anything, regardless of who they wronged for their personal greed and success, regardless of their reputation and beliefs.

These kinds of people were the worst viewed citizens in that time. Yet, even they came to John through the word of God seeking the answers on how to change their lives and be made new with God. They believed in John the Baptist as a man of God and a prophet. They believed God spoke through John and the guidance John gave was the only way to be saved. The guidance John gave was to make ready, repent and be prepared; confess their sins, and be baptized. John also told the people that there was one coming whose sandal strap John himself was not worthy to loose. He would bring forth the true baptism of the Holy Spirit. John of course was speaking about Jesus Christ. John was pouring his heart out to the people of the region to believe that the time of forgiveness of sins through the Messiah and savior was at hand. John's one purpose was to make people believe their savior was coming. This is He who hung on the cross for all of us to be saved and transformed—Jesus Christ! God gave the answer through John the Baptist to lead the people to Jesus Christ and believe He was the Savior!

Today's tax collectors are a diverse group made up of: alcoholics, drug addicts, prostitutes, drug dealers, adulterers, thieves, dishonest politicians, sex offenders, crooked businessmen, sexually immoralist, and gangs. This entire group is made up of individuals worried about themselves and what they lustfully desire in life to satisfy their needs and wants. They will do most anything and trample over most anyone to attain their objectives. I was one of these tax collectors before knowing Jesus Christ. There are many tax collectors today who will hear and respond to the cry of repentance and ask God, "What must I do?" We all need Jesus Christ! Only through believing in God's word and repentance in God's name can we attain the instructions of transformation needed to make us new. Our entire nation needs this call of repentance. We as a nation need to seek the words of God with a repenting heart if America has any hope of retaining mercy from God the Father and becoming new again!

Believe, believe, believe, and pray to God to strengthen your belief each and every day. Our transformation from this point on, needs to reflect Jesus Christ's teachings and life example He laid out for all of us through ultimate love. I want to touch on the baptist part of John the Baptist. At this stage of our Transformation, we are beginning to believe more and more daily. We are experiencing sustained peace and confidence God will not turn His back on us. After all, through honesty and repentance we should have confessed we were always the one who turned our back on God. I began being convicted in my heart to be baptized at this time. I wanted to proclaim Jesus Christ as my savior and be held accountable by not only God, but other fellow brothers and sisters of the new life in Christ I was given and had chosen. Several months later after becoming part of a church family, I did just that. I went to the Cedar River, not too far from our church, and was baptized in front of the whole congregation. Praise God, my wife was baptized with me that very day as well!

We had both been baptized previously—me at birth and my wife after our marriage and her conversion to my denomination. But baptism meant much more. When I was a baby, my parents did the right thing in baptizing me. It was really a baby dedication. It is a promise to God that they, as my parents, would raise me according to God's word and be godly examples for me. What did I have to do with that baptism? I was an infant with very few concerns—eat, sleep, get my diaper changed, stay warm, eat, and eat (I've always been fond of the eating part to this day). I felt drawn to be baptized shortly after accepting Christ into my heart and that feeling did not leave. I came to understand baptism through the scriptures and further believe it was a representation of Christ's death and resurrection into new life. I also believed my public baptism was a confession of the belief that through Christ's sacrifice and my repentance, I was dying to the old life of sin I had known and being reborn in new life with Christ—transformed!

We must believe this new life in Christ is a lifelong journey and decision. Our public baptism is a way to proclaim our belief and further please our Lord. I also believe that through my baptism, I was further opened to God's Holy Spirit and being prepared to understand the message He was about to show me!

## Believe in Jesus' Teachings

> If I have told you earthly things and you do not believe, how will you believe if I tell you heavenly things?
>
> —John 3:12

Listen to this verse! Read it again and truly let who it is who is asking it sink into your heart. This is Jesus Christ our Lord and Savior!

In this verse of scripture, Jesus is speaking with Nicodemus who was a member of the Pharisees (one sect of religious leaders of the Jews). Jesus is explaining that lest a man be born again, he can no way enter into the kingdom of God. Nicodemus asks Jesus, "Can a man enter into his mother's womb a second time and be born?" Jesus explains the rebirth of a man through the Spirit. Nicodemus asks, "How can these things be?" Jesus replies with the verse this chapter is focusing on from John 3:12. Jesus is telling Nicodemus, and all of us, that we must believe what He is teaching pertains to this life and this world to be able to have faith enough to believe and seek the kingdom of heaven to come.

Jesus is making it very clear at this point: our surrender and belief to God's word is the determining factor for our success in overcoming the trials of this world, and possessing the faith needed to believe the promises that God has in store for us in the next.

*3:12 Transformation* was birthed upon this very verse that came from John 3:12. When I awoke at 3:12 a.m. November 29, 2010, from the dream God had showed me, I felt a presence and communication never before known to me. My eyes were meant to be opened at that time and that moment of my life. I also had the thought 3:12 recovery in an instant, without even realizing what God was about to show me in the Bible. I had no idea the very verse He was pointing me to was indeed going to further brand that belief and presence I was sensing into my spirit. The reading of this scripture caused me to nearly faint. I remember this night as just yesterday and believe I always will. I believed Jesus Himself was giving a direct message to me—His broken sinner whom He had given mercy, grace, and salvation through the cross. I believed the calling upon my heart was given to me by God, and I believed God wished for this calling to become manifested through His Holy Spirit and my willingness to carry the message. I was willing, I was in awe, and I was in prayer with God, thanking Him for truly revealing Himself to me.

I should explain at this time the 3:12 recovery. After asking my partner, Larry, to join me in this ministry after much prayer and debate, we chose 3:12 Transformation as the only name to call this miraculous gift God has given us. God is transforming us through these Biblical verses and His Son! We will be made new and altered from what we have known before. We are being transformed into a new creation! We kicked around recovery, redemption, and transformation. Recovery presented two issues:

1. Recovery is the same person or entity in a repaired state.
2. Recovery is associated with every other get-well group on the planet.

Redemption was a close runner-up for the ministry name, but it resembled fixing and repairing the old man into a redeemed man. Now, I will hopefully never pass an opportunity at redemption of past mistakes and regrets, but redemption still did not cover the scope of God's plan Larry and I felt God had in store for us.

At this point, we are undergoing far more than recovery and redemption, we are being transformed in to a new creation through Jesus Christ! The success and timeline of this transformation is highly dependent upon our belief. Jesus is pleading with us to remove our beliefs of the perceptions we have lived our lives under, and follow His teachings. The gospels are a biography of the life of Jesus Christ and His teachings. Jesus advises us how to deal with and overcome every situation we will face in life. He also tells us in Luke 9:23 "If anyone desires to come after Me, let him deny himself, and take up his cross daily, and follow Me."

Deny ourselves? My life before surrender to Christ was nothing close to denial of myself. I occasionally made a sacrifice for a loved one but almost always with the intent of personal gain. I can honestly say that even when I had the best of intentions in mind, looking back, there was much selfishness involved. After some time as a true follower of Jesus Christ I began to believe what denial of oneself meant. God shows us time and time again through the scriptures. As I read the Bible and the gospels, I began to see Jesus not only performed numerous miracles and the ultimate sacrifice for us; He also left a blueprint for us to follow. This blueprint is through His teachings and actions. Jesus showed us how to pray, what to ask for, how to worship in spirit, defend ourselves against the enemy, and above all, to trust in Him and believe He will carry our burdens. Read the gospels and listen how many times Jesus tells us to have faith; do not be afraid and believe in Him. Our lives become so complicated and busy. We get carried away trying to solve problems, and as a result, take Jesus out of the picture.

We must strengthen our belief through God's word. As a result, our faith will continue to grow. When our belief and faith grow, we begin to take our worries and doubts to Jesus Christ at the first sign of unrest rather than falling into our lifelong routine of trying to control the situation by our own means. This is exactly what Christ is telling us in John 3:12. The Apostle Paul speaks it perfectly in Romans 12:2, "And do not be conformed to this world, but be Transformed by the renewing of your mind, that you may prove what is that good and acceptable and perfect will of God."

How do we renew our minds? Well, we have been given forgiveness and salvation. We have looked at our past and taken responsibility for our wrongs. We have confessed our remorse and repentance to God and asked Jesus into our hearts. We have been freed from the chains of bondage we have known, released from the burden of guilt and shame, and have been given new hope and peace never before known. Our house is clean for the first time in years. Where do we go from here? In the Gospel of Matthew 12:43–45, Jesus tells us of a man whose house has been cleaned and put in order. Unfortunately, the man leaves his house empty and fails to fill it properly. As a result, the man's state eventually becomes worse than ever before. What we are being taught in these verses is to fill our clean house God has provided. We need to fill it with God's word. Fill it with prayer and meekness. Fill our house with faith and belief that our transformation is underway and will be completed by the promise given to us by God.

If we fail to fill our house, which is our spirit, we will again leave plenty of room for the enemy to move in once again, and again fall into bondage once delivered from. Our situations will be far worse than ever before experienced. I failed to fill my house many times in life, and my fall was greater each time. We can always lower our bottom. Jesus is telling us that it will no longer happen if we believe in Him and His teachings.

On the topic of believing in Jesus, let's look closer at what I believe the confession truly means.

> In the beginning was the Word, and the Word was with God, and the Word was God
>
> John 1:1

> And the Word became flesh and dwelt among us, and we beheld His glory, the glory as of the only begotten of the Father, full of grace and truth
>
> John 1:14

> "He who believes in Him is not condemned; but he who does not believe is condemned already, because he has not believed in the name of the only begotten Son of God"
>
> John 3:18

When looking at 1:1 and 1:14 of the Gospel of John, Jesus was the name given to the Word of God. When we accept Jesus Christ as our Lord and savior, are we not confessing that we believe and will live as Jesus taught us? Now let's look at John 3:18. When I confess my faith in Jesus, I am truly confessing my belief and obedience to the Word of God. The Word of God is the Bible from cover to cover. We must be obedient to the Word's (Jesus') teaching throughout the entire Bible. We must believe in the total package, believe in the whole Word, and follow the plan to its entirety the best we can with guidance from the Word!

Too often we like to pick and choose what parts of the Bible we will be obedient in. This is generally based upon what responses will be from others or perhaps what our peers believe. We settle for quick gains and comforts rather than sustained perseverance. Jesus is making things very clear for us in John 3:12: Our belief and trust in His way, whether it is the easy way or not, must become resolved! His way is definitely the righteous way which leads to eternal gains and comforts!

My belief exploded off the charts the morning of November 29, 2010, at 3:12 a.m. What I once felt unattainable became reality. God will give each and every one of us the surge of faith needed to strengthen our belief. God's timing is perfect and precise. We merely need to stay surrendered, speak with God as often as we can in prayer, read and study God's word as much as possible, and remain willing to be taught. One more thing, when we see and hear from God—believe!

## Faith in Christ

> In whom we have boldness and access with confidence through Him.
>
> —Ephesians 3:12

Boldness and confidence—Ephesians 3:12 is explaining how Jesus Christ became the way to manifest God's plan for all of us. Through Jesus we can begin to know the wisdom of God, and His mysteries may be revealed. Jesus becomes our great intercessor to the throne of

God Himself. All our prayers and requests are to be given to Jesus Christ, our Lord. We are transforming our lives into true disciples of Christ. We need not to take our requests and tribulations to any other source than Jesus Christ and God, our Father. My faith grows every day along this journey. I pray within my spirit to Jesus, God, and the Holy Spirit as much as I consciously can. I also believe, we can be praying to God in spirit even when we are unaware of the fact. Jesus truly dwells within our hearts. Romans 8:26 tells us that the Holy Spirit makes intercession for us with groaning that cannot be uttered. Through our faith and belief, we can determine how much of ourselves we give for Christ's dwelling and guidance of the Holy Spirit. Belief and faith are so critical! Our faith will grow the more we read God's word.

> So then faith comes by hearing, and hearing by the word of God.
>
> (Romans 10:17)

> For we walk by faith, not by sight.
>
> (2 Corinthians 5:7)

> Now faith is the substance of things hoped for, the evidence of things not seen.
>
> (Hebrews 11:1)

> But without faith it is impossible to please Him, for he who comes to God must believe that He is, and that He is a rewarder of those who diligently seek Him.
>
> (Hebrews 11:6)

> For by Grace you have been saved through faith, and that not of yourselves; it is the gift of God.
>
> (Ephesians 2:8)

These are just a few scriptures that speak of faith throughout the Bible. But do you not see the trend they are setting? It's the plea of God to believe! Faith is belief that God will do for us what we could never do. These verses show clearly that our faith and belief grow through God's word. We then are instructed to walk according to those words with the belief that they are true and righteous. God tells us to see the hopes and dreams of the end result and believe them. God tells us none of this is possible without the belief and faith required from us to whole heartedly seek Him. And finally, God reminds us that this was a gift to begin with! We did not earn this salvation, it was granted to us according to some small increment of belief we chose to surrender to.

Somewhere in our wretched souls, which we possessed before surrender to God, there had to be a small seed of faith that brought us to this point. Just remember it was a gift! I often thought surrender was the main part of anyone's recovery and their chances at long term success. Now, I would say that surrender is the biggest part of recovery, but belief is the largest building block along the way of transformation! The transformation God has in store is requiring of saint-like faith. But that is exactly what each and every one of us are when we surrender our lives over to God and ask Jesus into our hearts. God's Holy Spirit will supply the faith needed to believe. Our great intercessor, Jesus Christ, will hear our requests and lay them before the throne of heaven for us. We are not in this battle alone. We never were. If so, we would not have the salvation we now know.

At the end of "Believe," and speaking of battles Christ has delivered us from, I think of the battle of Armageddon to come. I realize, at this point of transformation, many have been involved or are involved in our own personal Armageddon.

Revelation tells us of the final war, Armageddon. This war will take place on earth between Jesus, His angels, and saints and Satan and the forces of wickedness.

But do we ever stop to think of our personal Armageddon (the battle which positions us on the side of Christ to begin with)?

Not all Christians will go through the same degree of warfare and battle, but it's safe to say all will encounter this time in their life when our spirit (through the guidance of the Holy Spirit) becomes involved in spiritual Armageddon which will anchor our position for the Biblical Armageddon to come: the time when our savior Jesus Christ returns and forever abolishes the evil of this present world. During our personal Armageddon, the enemy will come at our weaknesses and strengths. This season is usually going to leave us in the most vulnerable state we could imagine. Any shield of faith we may or may not have had up to this point will be greatly compromised. Rather than being upright and prepared to stop the fiery arrows, our shields will be all but fallen completely off our grips. We will be as exhausted objects of humanity, on our knees, with what little means of strength remaining merely trying to lift our chins off our chest, but petrified to see what lies ahead. Then we present ourselves as the perfect target for Satan to no longer launch fiery arrows but to project the nuclear warhead of desolation directly into our souls. We are truly defeated, bewildered, and longing to cease the tragedy of hopelessness which keeps playing through our minds.

On our own strength and resources we cannot rely. Our best efforts and thoughts will not avail us anything. We are truly under the Armageddon of our life which we will experience upon this earth…the one which will determine which side we will be on for the future Armageddon in which our Lord has revealed to us through His word. Then, during the midst of this onslaught, we are reminded of a love which we cannot explain. We are drawn to a wellspring of perseverance which is not of our resources. We sense a greater purpose to our lives than the current mourning we are undergoing. We see shadows of promises made, blessings to come, and victories ahead…we see all these things and are made aware of all these emotions through the image of a lamb upon an altar. The altar is in the form of a cross.

We make our allegiance with that lamb, to rely upon Him, regardless of the future we face. We have been given victory over the enemy! The warhead traveling straight for our soul has been blocked by the altar in the form of the cross, which had always been our shield of faith from the beginning. God has chosen us so we at this particular time of our personal Armageddon could choose Him. Choose to serve Him, choose to obey Him, and most of all…choose to fight for Him in the likeness of His Son. We carry this life battle with our fellow brothers and sisters and their personal Armageddon which they are facing. We will carry this fight into the next life as well. The battle in which we will fight alongside our savior when the evils of this world are defeated for good!

To God, the Father of our Savior Jesus Christ, be the glory of all our individual Armageddons and the final one to come!

Continued growth and knowledge in Jesus Christ will lead to more faith and belief. The Holy Spirit will supply peace and understanding never known before. What do you choose to believe in right now? If you are a new Christian embarking on this journey, I ask you to stop and ask yourself that very question. Do you believe that Jesus Christ will hear your requests? Do you believe you are being remade new, transformed, and given a purpose? Do you believe Jesus Christ will see you through to the end? I cannot answer these questions for you. I can answer the question for myself and will promise you, I believe the answer with all my heart! But I will refer to the Bible, the Holy Word of God for the answer, and you can too!

To sum it up, "Being confident of this very thing, that He who has begun a good work in you will complete it until the day of Jesus Christ" (Philippians 1:6).

## Believe

*3:12 Transformation*

In your words, what do you believe God is saying to you in Jeremiah 3:12?

____________________________________________

____________________________________________

____________________________________________

____________________________________________

Do you believe you have heard God's calling of repentance? Are you willing to do whatever necessary to answer your call?

____________________________________________

____________________________________________

____________________________________________

____________________________________________

What does being a believer in Jesus Christ mean to you?

____________________________________________

____________________________________________

____________________________________________

____________________________________________

How do you picture yourself becoming bolder and more prayerful in Jesus?

________________________________________

________________________________________

________________________________________

________________________________________

Do you have a personal Armageddon testimony? Explain how you have been or believe you will be delivered.

________________________________________

________________________________________

________________________________________

________________________________________

LIVE
BELIEVE
SURRENDER

# LIVE

## God's Individual Plan for Each of Us

> "Behold, I have done according to your words; see, I have given you a wise and understanding heart, so that there has not been anyone like you before you, nor shall any like you arise after you."
>
> —1 Kings 3:12

We have surrendered to God and our belief in Him is growing stronger day by day. But what is this really leading up to? We are being transformed into a new creation and therefore, a new way of life and purpose for life will manifest itself as well. The third phase of 3:12 Transformation is to "Live"—that is exactly what God will be teaching us with the verses involved. The "Live" phase contains more scriptural verses than any other phase of 3:12 Transformation. The explanation for this is simple: we lived the majority of our lives wrongfully seeking and attempting to control our destinies. Now we must be spiritually guided to understand God's destiny for us. We must also be guided daily to learn how to live that destiny in Christ.

We will be shown new ways of thinking, acting, giving, and understanding. All we have known has been from the human viewpoint, not from God's viewpoint. We will begin to see God's infinite wisdom and grace that we will base our new foundation in Christ upon. God will reveal this wisdom and direction to us through His word and Holy Spirit. God will also show us during this stage our true uniqueness and individuality and the intimate relationship He desires to have with us. This is exactly what we see in 1 Kings 3:12.

Some background to this verse: King Solomon, king of Israel and builder of the first temple in Jerusalem, has a dream where God speaks to him. God is pleased with Solomon and says to him in the dream, "Ask! What shall I give you?" Solomon thanks God for His mercy, grace, and kindness he has received and the kindness shown his father King David. Solomon asks for something that I would venture to say, not too many humans would ask for. Solomon asks God for an understanding heart to judge God's people and discernment between good and evil. In short, he asks God for wisdom, knowledge, and God's presence with him. This request pleases God, and God replies to him with the verse this chapter is based upon—1 Kings 3:12.

In God's reply to Solomon, He not only grants the request, but God takes it much further and tells him there will never be, nor has there ever been another king as Solomon. God wants Solomon to understand without a shadow of a doubt that he has an individual calling and relationship with God that no other human created can have. God is telling us that there will never be another Solomon, but also, there will never be another you! God gave Solomon his request because it was from a pure, humble, and grateful heart. God also gave Solomon what he did not ask for. He gave him riches and honor that were unmatched by all kings before or after as well. Now, we should not expect to become rich and famous, but we can expect God to show us what our individual calling will be. The calling we receive may be similar to others; but our role for God cannot be fulfilled by any other human. It is our calling and ours alone. It is our commission, and when God reveals it to us, we will know. This is the level of intimacy the creator of the universe wants to have with the humble, beautiful you!

When we give all we know to give to Jesus Christ, our Lord and Savior, we will be shown how to live! God's Holy Spirit when sought, will lead us through life on a daily basis. We must seek with a willing and pure heart. It is really no longer about us; it is about living a life set forth by the example of Jesus Christ, and it is about striving to please God. All the emphasis on belief is leading up to this very stage of transformation. God has freed us. Now it is time to live for Him and take the path in life God will send us on. Be at peace; God Himself will walk along this path with us and fight our battles for us. All that is required is faith and remain surrendered and let Him fight those battles. Jesus came to give us life and life abundantly! That message is not just for our eternal life in heaven, but also for our life we are living today. We did not give ourselves to God merely to live out our days in isolation, mediocrity, and boredom. We give our lives over to God with the hope of better days ahead and dreams of things to come. Jesus Christ died for us to begin experiencing that life of new hope as soon as we ask Him into our heart, and repent for our sins.

God will prepare in your heart a wise and loving new creation to replace the foolish soul of the world that once occupied His temple. You will be shown how to live by God. You will begin to sense wisdom and discernment through God's Holy Spirit for protection against temptations and snares of the world. Our old lives were filled with sin. Sin leads to death. We are given Life! We are given life abundantly! Seek God's intimacy and plans He has for you. Ask Him very clearly in prayer and not just one time. Humbly ask God daily to show the path for you to follow and that your individual calling be made known through His Spirit. I can witness to the fact that my own calling was given very clearly to me by God. I am following that calling through the ministry of 3:12 Transformation and with this book. I can also witness that I asked for the wisdom and knowledge of what the calling would be for several months leading up to God's revelation. Don't you think King Solomon's request was contained in his heart and prayers long before God ever asked him to give it? Through our honest living for God, we will lose the spontaneous requests for quick satisfaction, and let our true desires of our heart come to light through

God's marvelous timing. Do not be discouraged if you do not get your answer as soon as you would like. You may even mistake your calling as the calling of God for a time or two. It's okay. We want to please our heavenly Father, and this may lead to some overzealous reactions at times. Ask yourself this: If God did not spare His Son and Spirit when we called upon Him during our lives of sin and despair, do you think He will not respond now that we are seeking Him as best we can? Be patient; you are learning to live all over again. Just believe how much God loves you, and He will make known to each and every one of us His individual plan for only us.

In ending this chapter, I have one more question to ask you. Do you surrender, believe, and accept living this life and calling that God has for you? If *you* do not, then tell me who can replace you in the eyes of God?

## BUILD UPON THE FOUNDATION OF CHRIST

> Now if anyone builds on this foundation with gold, silver, precious stones, wood, hay, straw.
>
> —1 Corinthians 3:12

In the beginning of chapter 1, I spoke on a foundation in Christ. This is the subject of "Live" we are going to look into this chapter. We are God's building! "For we are God's fellow workers; you are God's field, you are God's building" (1 Corinthians 3:9). A building for

God needs a rock-solid foundation. In the "Live" phase of 3:12 Transformation, our journey depends upon the foundation we will build. Stone-by-stone, we must lay this foundation in our belief and faith in Jesus Christ and His teachings. In 1 Peter 2:6 it is quoted from scriptures, "Behold, I lay in Zion a chief cornerstone, elect, precious, and he who believes on Him will by no means be put to shame." Jesus Christ is our cornerstone. All we do must be anchored upon and adjacent to our cornerstone. We are rebuilding our house; we are rebuilding our spiritual temples. Our foundation is built upon our obedience to God. If we are to live a godly life through Jesus Christ, we must be founded upon Jesus Christ. Equip yourself with the proper tools to construct the foundation—faith, kindness, love, hope, good works, perseverance, and selflessness. We need to give ourselves to Jesus Christ and His teachings to learn and attain these tools.

Our foundation will support our entire house we are building. Jesus is not only the cornerstone but also our master builder and blueprint if we give ourselves to Him.

Jesus tells us in Matthew 7:24–27 how a wise man builds his house upon a rock. When the floods came and winds blew, the man's house remained. He also tells us how a foolish man builds his house on the sand. When the winds blew and the floods came the man's house fell. He also tells us the fall of the house was great. Jesus is telling us to build our foundation and house upon Him. When we do this, our house through Jesus Christ will stand up against the attacks of the world, tribulations of life, and the snares of the enemy. Storms will come, but our house will remain! If we choose to build our house upon a foundation we have created through the cares of this world, we are choosing to build upon the sand once again. When the winds blow and the floods come through the trials in life, our house will fall! How can a foundation that is not founded in stone survive? It cannot!

Our foundation and house we build in this life is not merely for this world. Our true foundation will be tested in the life to come—the day we all come before Jesus Christ. 1 Corinthians 3:12–13 tell us in that day, each one's work will become clear and shall be revealed by fire. The fire will test each one's work of what sort it is. Our works from this moment until that day will be the assembling of our foundation and construction of our house. There is nothing that we can build without Jesus Christ that will withstand the fire.

I built a house upon a sand foundation time and time again throughout my life. I labored upon the foundation with anxiety, fear, resentment, and doubt. Each time when the wind blew and flood waters rose, my house was laid to waste. It truly became a house of desolation. I blindly skipped past the cornerstone that is Jesus Christ in the foundation with every house leading up to surrender of my life to Christ. If Jesus would have returned, and the day of judgment taken place during any of the previous houses I had constructed, my house would have been consumed by fire. Nothing would have endured the fire of God. The foundation, if it would have remained, would have been a bleak example of man's pride and foolishness. Thankfully, God's fire came into my soul before I came before Him on the day of reckoning. God gave me forgiveness and love. God gave me peace and courage. God gave me His Son. Through the Holy Spirit, my soul was consumed by the fire of God, and I was convicted to build one more house. Also through God's Holy Spirit, I was given humility and wisdom to call upon Jesus Christ to be the foundation of my house and works that I would labor upon.

That is what 1 Corinthians 3:12 is telling us. Our foundation in Christ should reflect a life led by Christ. Any and all materials need to come from God's word. We cannot begin to build a structure that will endure into eternity without an eternal foundation! I want my house supported upon a foundation where my wife can feel secure, my children will feel safe and loved, and my soul will be at peace throughout the storms that will arise. We are given an opportunity to strengthen our foundation each and every day through our example we set in life. Let your example be clearly seen as a follower of Jesus Christ! Build upon love, kind acts, and your faith daily. Pray that your foundation be made strong and stand up to the fire on the day of the Lord.

Our building of our foundation will go on forever. Devote the time and obedience to ensure that through Christ it will endure forever. Now, there will be times when our foundations will be tested. We may see areas of our foundation we are building upon that have no use for God's kingdom. We are humans still, and on occasion may try to fit a selfish stone or two into our walls. God will show us when there is a stone that cannot fit with His foundation He is assembling through us. The foundations we will build are for God! Be careful to seek spiritual guidance in performing God's work and not our own. I will use myself as an example again. If my foundation, ministry, and house be built upon the foundation and will of God, it will stand. If my foundation, ministry, and house are being built for my will, all will perish. I believe it to be of God and for God! I can assure you, I still have trials and tribulations in life and you will have your own share also. Do not lose faith, some days will be glorious, and some downright horrible. I am confident the majority will fall in the middle of the two and be filled with peace in knowing God loves us and will guide us. We are laboring upon a foundation intended to last forever. We will not complete this foundation overnight.

## Continued Growth: We're Not Perfect

> Not that I have already attained, or am already perfected; but I press on, that I may lay hold of that for which Christ Jesus has also laid hold of me.
>
> —Philippians 3:12

God has truly given us an outline of rebirth and transformation to follow. We are building upon our foundation and striving daily to improve, perhaps even aiming to be perfect. Philippians 3:12 tells us to press on and fight the good fight. It also tells us to keep things in perspective. We are not perfect; we are merely broken sinners who have been given grace and mercy through Jesus Christ. Our pursuit toward this perfection in Christ will last the rest of our mortal lives and is only available because of Jesus making it available to us. We will make beautiful changes by the grace of God as we live this new life in Christ. Be careful not to fall under the illusion that all has been done by our own individual resources and righteousness.

"Fight the good fight of faith, lay hold on eternal life, to which you were also called and have confessed the good confession in the presence of many witnesses" (1 Timothy 6:12). This is exactly what our continued growth in Christ is all about—eternal life. Through our humble confession of the good news in Christ, we are building our faith and planting seeds for God. These seeds, by the grace of God, may one day be used to further enlarge God's kingdom and glory. We are pressing on to lay hold of our eternal life with Christ by confessing what Christ has done for us. This is done by living a life of faith and seeking further intimacy with God. We have not been forgiven by our own power, resources, and glory; all we have has come through the one who is perfect—Jesus Christ. We will struggle and, at times, maybe regress. We will doubt, have moments of lost faith, and have attacks of anxiety and fear. We may believe, for a time, we are not able to complete this journey we have begun traveling on. We are right; we cannot complete this on our own. But we do not have to. We, shall I say you, are chosen! You were first convicted and led by the holy, perfect Jesus Christ.

We do not have to be perfect. We only need to press on through the good times and the bad knowing that Christ will carry us through to the end. We merely need to continue asking to lay hold of Jesus Christ and God's will for us.

I am not perfect. As an alcoholic and forgiven sinner, I must look back at the life I led and the way I handled disappointments in the past. I wanted issues resolved immediately. I wanted my pain and suffering removed as quickly as possible. I wanted to be the perfect example of a capable man who could attain resolution by his own resources. I also wanted others to know of my brilliant wisdom and how I fixed all things that had been amiss. I certainly was not perfect, but desired to be. I felt any less desire was underachieving. I lived a life of fear, bondage of my thoughts, and futile attempts toward perfection.

This book, *3:12 Transformation*, is showing us, through the divine guidance of God, a new way to live. I will no longer live all-in for today, although I will give all I have for today. My thoughts of attaining perfection in this life have been replaced with attaining grace for my eternal life. I will give Jesus Christ glory every time I lead a fellow brother or sister to His kingdom, and not act as though I am the authority that set them free. Thank God He does not expect perfection out of us as soon as we surrender to His will. If it were a rule that had to be followed to stay in the mercy of God, then there would be very, very few people in heaven—if by chance you would make it there to see. "For by Grace you have been saved through Faith, and that not of yourselves; it is the gift of God" (Ephesians 2:8). This new life in Christ is a gift. Jesus hung upon the cross for us when we were all sinners and broken. He will give grace and mercy for us now and also, when we fail to be as perfect as we would like.

Boast not in ourselves or our accomplishments. Boast in Jesus Christ and the sacrifice, forgiveness, and victory He has in you! "For I determined not to know anything among you except Jesus Christ and Him crucified" (1 Corinthians 2:2). This is our testimony; this is our witness to spread to others. We have been saved. We do not need to be perfect—we only need to further seek the one who saved us and live our life as an example of His love. Further seek God's wisdom and gifts of the spirit He will bestow upon you. The devil tries to attack me in this area to this very day. It is so easy to once again place expectations upon myself that I cannot reach. I will judge and criticize my actions. Did I do enough? Did I not do enough? Satan wants me questioning my worth and salvation once again. Satan wants you to question the very same thing. Remember, *Satan is a liar!*

Different denominations have different views on perfection. I will not enter into that discussion in this book. I only want to tell you this: live your life in an attempt to be perfect and holy before the Lord, but do not give up when you realize that may never happen. God will use victories and disappointments to further show us His purpose for our lives. We are a work in progress as we see in Philippians 3:12. Strive for perfection, but we'll never get there. But God's Son, He is perfect, and your sin He did bear!

# Become Kind, Meek, and Merciful

> Therefore, as the elect of God, holy and beloved, put on tender mercies, kindness, humility, meekness, longsuffering.
>
> —Colossians 3:12

Living our lives as an elect of God? Just what exactly is that saying to us? Colossians 3:12 tells us, as the elect of God we are holy and beloved. It tells us to live life mercifully, kindly, humbly, meekly, and with perseverance. The definition of elect in this format is: those who have heard, believed, and been saved through Jesus Christ; and those who have been set apart by the Holy Spirit of God. At this stage of our transformation, if we are seeking God with a true and pure heart we should not only believe we are the elect, but begin to live in a manner that reinforces this. Our light should be shining more and more for others to see.

Let's look at how we lived life before becoming the elect of God, and what fruits came forth as a result. My example may relate to many other people. Colossians 3:12 says, "Put on tender mercies." Be forgiving towards others. I never allowed myself to forgive those I felt harmed or wronged me. I believed in my mind I must keep my guard up at all times. Only a fool forgave an enemy. I believed an enemy would more than likely cause harm to me again. Then, I would only have myself to blame. Sometimes these people were not even enemies. They could be family members, co-workers, children, etc. I believed and lived under the perception that my forgiveness and mercy towards others was a sign of weakness. Forgiveness also acknowledged I was not perfect and could possibly need forgiveness, as well. What a horrible thought in the mind of a man trying to be God himself. How could the person who hurt me be made to suffer if I forgive them? They should feel the same pain I felt because of their actions.

This verse also says to become kind and humble. Kindness was only shown if I believed people were no threat to me. If you haven't gathered by now, I pretty well thought everyone was a threat to me. I had moments of kindness but usually only to ensure kindness in return. True kindness with no expectations of a return upon investment was seldom performed. I had many cases of being utterly humiliated in life, but no true sense of humility or trust in God existed. Humility was always something to be ashamed of in my mind. Colossians 3:12 also speaks about meekness and long-suffering. Meekness was weakness in my way of thinking. I had to be strong and viewed that way by family, friends, and all society. Longsuffering is a way of saying perseverance, patience, and faith for better days to come. Not a common theme to a man as myself who wanted everything fixed now, immediately, and exactly the way I thought it should be. Hopefully, you see just how blindly and fearfully I lived my life. My fruits reflected my life and manner in which I lived. Among these fruits were alcoholism, fear, strife, remorse, deceitfulness, lack of self control, selfishness, shame, and despair.

Our fruits are what abound from us through our actions and way of life. Our fruits are a sign of what our tree is soaking up through our roots. Think of your soul as the tree. The beliefs we have in life, our spiritual foundation, and our values and morals are the roots. From what source do we choose to grow our roots into for the nutrients we need to sustain our tree? If our source be the world and the perceptions of success in the world, your fruits probably have a similar taste and appearance as the fruits I brought forth for many years. If our source be Jesus Christ and God's word and Holy Spirit, expect much different results. Our heavenly Father has told us what these fruits will look like, and how others will know you are the elect of God.

> But the fruit of the Spirit is love, joy, peace, longsuffering, kindness, goodness, faithfulness, gentleness, self-control. Against such there is no law. And those who are Christ's have crucified the flesh with its passions and desires.
>
> Galatians 5:22–24

This book, *3:12 Transformation,* shows us a new way to live according to God's word. Jesus Christ set the perfect example for us to follow. Galatians 5:22–24 is describing the fruits of the spirit that will manifest through our transforming life in Jesus Christ. God's word will grow from within our hearts and souls and develop a root system that will tap into God's Holy Spirit. True kindness and meekness will be known and demonstrated. True mercy and forgiveness will begin to seem like a possibility and a desire. Humility will be displayed in our ability to trust God and His will for us and not attempting to be God. We will begin to accept circumstances that are unpleasant with the faith and belief God will deliver us, and our relationship with Him will grow during those times of trials. These circumstances may be debts left to pay from our lives of sin we have known or could be new trials awaiting us in the future. Just remember and believe that God will deliver you. You are the elect of God! Galatians 5:22-24 joins perfectly with Colossians 3:12 and further explains why God stresses to us when in early stages of our transformation to rejoice and do good works (Ecclesiastes 3:12). God begins to cut away the roots that fed from the sinful world and replant roots that feed off His holy word.

## Increasing Love for Others

> And may the Lord make you increase and abound in love to one another and to all, just as we do to you.
>
> —1 Thessalonians 3:12

The words in 1 Thessalonians 3:12 speak of abounding love toward one another. It speaks of the Lord giving the increase for our love to abound toward all men. The relationship with our Lord, Jesus Christ is the increase needed to make this possible. As we live our life seeking

Jesus' teachings and then put them into action by our example, others will see the fruit and know to whom we belong. Jesus Christ set the example we all need to follow to receive the fruits of the Spirit and a love that grows toward all mankind—true love, not the love we have known while in bondage to the world and sin. True love is explained in 1 Corinthians 13. Love was always a selfish action to me before I knew Christ as my Lord and Savior. I judged love by what someone was willing to do for me, not by what I was willing to sacrifice for another. My love was lustful, prideful, controlling, and selfish. My love at that time sounds a lot like fear and low self-esteem to me from today's viewpoint.

Jesus Christ set the bar for love. Out of love, He took the cross for all of us—the most selfless act in the history of mankind. Christ sacrificed for all of us because of the ferocious love of the Father. As we live a life founded on Jesus Christ, we will perform acts of love, selflessness, and kindness we could have never performed before. Our fruits will also be distributed to all those we come into contact with. Our examples of living a life based upon the example of Christ will shine as a light for all to see. The fruits of the spirit will illuminate our lights brighter over time. We can become loving, truly loving. We will not only learn to show love to those closest to us but in time, also to those we believed farthest away. Jesus Christ told us, "By this all will know that you are My disciples, if you have love for one another" (John 13:35). As a disciple of Christ and to truly transform our old man-of-sin into a new creation, we must be crucified along with Christ.

We must die to our old life, and be reborn into our new life. Death to fear, guilt, pride, and selfishness we have known; life to mercy, kindness, humility, meekness, patience, and above all, love.

## Focus on God's Calling

> Now those who are such we command and exhort through our Lord, Jesus Christ that they work in quietness and eat their own bread.
>
> —2 Thessalonians 3:12

Now we are entering into an area of "Live" that will require some deeper reflection and honesty of ourselves, along with added prayer. The verse from 2 Thessalonians 3:12 is guiding us to focus on our calling and direction from the Lord. Work in quietness and eat our own bread. What are we meant to see with this verse? Before my new life in Christ, I had no knowledge of what this example of living meant. I was focusing on what my calling was in my mind; I was also telling everyone else what my calling was, and what I felt their calling was. I was in everyone else's business and usually so consumed with plotting my victories, and what others needed for their victories. There was no peace or direction for any involved. I was blind to the calling God had for me and not at all willing to eat the meal He had prepared. I lived entangled in the thoughts of busyness and unrest in conquest to control not only my life, but everyone else's lives as well.

I also was occupied a big part of the day on outsmarting, out-calculating, and out-manipulating by those I felt threatened. I spent many a sleepless night with details from conversations, interactions, and appearances from others controlling my thoughts. I believed that if I could figure out the questions in my mind, as if some puzzle of wisdom that would place me in position of holding all the cards of knowledge, then all things could be made right. There was seldom a quiet moment in my mind. I was good at presenting the perception that I was calm, cool, and collected, but that was a lifelong rehearsal I acted out as a seasoned actor on the stage. My bread-and-plate set in front of me was by my own making through endless expectations I created in my mind. I never felt satisfied after consuming what I had prepared for myself. I focused on my perceptions, not on God's calling.

The verse in 2 Thessalonians 3:12 is telling us to seek, perform, and be content on the calling God has for us. God is our provider. God places the plate in front of us that He wishes us to eat at this time of our life and this stage of our transformation. Jesus Christ tells us in the gospels, "I am the bread of life" (John 6:35). Our bread is spiritual and rationed to us in measures of faith that coincides with our current calling and season we are involved in. Now, at times, we may not be thrilled about the bread we are eating that is placed before us. Sometimes we need to go through some valleys in order to reach the mountain. The valleys can represent seasons in life where we do not see much spiritual growth. We may even question if our growth has ended, or worse yet, began to regress. Do not be afraid. God has different lessons that we must learn further, removing of the old to usher in the new. If we stand fast to our faith, and live the life of a believer and a doer, we will have plenty of times with the Lord on the mountaintops. These times will present a plentiful feast provided by our Father that will satisfy our souls.

Be careful not to give into the attacks of Satan. He will try to cloud our vision and once again, return us to micromanaging our calling and everyone else's around us. As a result, we will be spinning our wheels and going backwards. We will accomplish nothing for God and usually realize this fact after a sound humbling we will put ourselves through. We all have a different calling as we have seen in 1 Kings 3:12. We need to reassure God will lead us throughout the entire task at hand. Let our minds be at peace and perform the calling God has called us into at the current time. "Not that I speak in regard to need, for I have learned in whatever state I am, to be content" (Philippians 4:11). Be content with God's plan even when it does not match up with your time schedule or train of thought. Rejoice and do good for God. Be at peace and quietly accept what God provides. There will be plenty of times when our Father will give more than we can hold as well!

## Lead as Christ has Shown Us

> Let deacons be the husbands of one wife, ruling their children and their own houses well.
>
> —1 Timothy 3:12

Once we further accept living as Christ has shown, we can become resolved to fulfill the position He has placed us in. The verse on 1 Timothy 3:12 speaks on deacons (elders of the church) and how they are to live. We may not be a deacon of our church at this point, but we are in a position for God nonetheless. It makes no difference what that position may be at this time—we all have one. We also have scriptural guidance that leads us by God's word in all areas. For me, I am in the position of a husband, father, and son. I am also an employee and a member of a church. God's word gives one example after another for me to follow in order to fulfill my part in all these relationships He has placed me in. As a husband, I am told in Ephesians 5:23–33 to love my wife and sacrifice for her—just as Christ sacrificed Himself for His church. Ephesians 6 instructs me how to treat my children, parents, employer, and anyone who works for me. These are just a few examples of the numerous examples that guide us throughout the Bible on our actions as a follower of Christ.

The point I am trying to make is this: we all have responsibilities that we are to fulfill no matter our position in life. As a father, there had been a change taking place in my home since I become a follower of Jesus Christ and recognized the changes that were required of me. I am the spiritual leader of my house. This is my God-given blessing, as well as God-given responsibility. "But as for me and my house, we will serve the Lord" (Joshua 24:15). This is a wonderful verse from Joshua—but it is also a way of life we need to adhere to, not just a quote or as mere words with no follow-up intentions.

Dads, who do we have to blame when we hear our children use explicit sexual words amongst their friends and siblings? If there are any television shows at our homes that promote this conduct, we can start by blaming ourselves. There are parental locks we can put on our television stations that makes it impossible to watch the filth in our own home. We can communicate to our children that minds filled with all things ungodly, will lead to ungodly things. If we face a decision to miss church and play in the baseball tournament every Sunday, how do we expect our families to prioritize church now or any time in the future? If we spend all our time watching television and sports, how do we show our children to be involved with helping others? It is sad to say, but this is radical thinking in this world today:

- *You would deprive your children from that.*
- *Johnny's Dad lets him watch this show.*
- *I am too tired to go to church.*
- *Honey, can't we get this new car, ours is 2 years old.*
- *I deserve some me time, I worked hard all week.*

This is the mentality we are up against today. This was never God's mentality, and still is not.

Each one of us is faced with leading a life that sets an example for others. It is our choice to set the example God has already scripted for us. Cycles must be broken if future generations are to avoid the same miserable outcome we have faced before knowing Christ. God is giving us new life. Along with a new life, new actions must follow. We will meet great resistance when we begin to live for God as He has instructed us to. Be expecting it and stand firm. When children are involved, we need to explain why we are leading as we are. This gives us a wonderful opportunity to truly speak with them on our faith and salvation. We are not to become self-righteous judges with this phase of "Live". We can accomplish this with patience and love. Over time, those around you will see your consistency and may even become curious about this new life you have chosen.

We can lead with strength and still display love. We can respect God's word and still remain respectful to those around us. Whatever position we are in, we can live a life based upon the convictions of our heart. By this time in our transformation, our hearts will be convicted in pleasing and honoring God. Pray God will give strength and encouragement needed to accomplish this new Life. Pray God will speak through you in the position of life you hold. It all starts with each one of us. Do we wish to fall back into the life of compromise and negligence to our creator and His plans for us? If we do, we fail God in this new life of salvation and glimpse of grace He has offered. We cannot pick and choose which scriptures we like and which scriptures to pass on because of how the world will respond. We not only fail our God, we fail all those around us as well.

Husbands, do you want to fail your wife and become another casualty in the long death of marriage this world has become numb to? Dads, do you want to fail your children and set another example of a father consumed with the world for your children to one day repeat? Employees, do you want to work honestly and respectfully for the blessings and job God provides through your employer, or slip into another case of entitlement, mediocrity, and constant strife towards your career? We need to lead by the example of Jesus Christ. We are given a new life, a new hope, and the same responsibility we always had just never responded to.

This phase will require further trust and communication through prayer with God. This area of change in life will not be easy. God promises us, He will guide us by the Holy Spirit and supply our every need. God also promises us that the world will attack us and persecute us. The world may even hate us for our faith and beliefs. In the next chapter, we will dive into this subject much deeper, and prepare ourselves for the trials that lie ahead.

## Persecutions and Trials

> Yes, and all who desire to live godly in Christ Jesus will suffer persecution.
>
> —2 Timothy 3:12

When we are not only hearing the word of God but also living the words of God, our new life in Christ will be very rewarding for the mind, body, and soul. We will grow stronger in faith and further in Christ each day we focus upon God's calling for us. We will begin to truly be an example of the elect of God. God's Holy Spirit will separate us from the rest of the world and how we live life. The verse in 2 Timothy 3:12 tells us, if we live our life as Jesus Christ taught us, we will suffer persecution. These persecutions will come in many different forms and from various places. Some persecutions will come from where we least expect, and from whom we least expect. Others will try to discourage, downplay, and disregard our faith in Christ. We will be under attack on a constant basis when we start becoming a voice for Christ.

Jesus speaks to His apostles and those around Him in Luke 21:17 and tells them, "And you will be hated by all for my name's sake." Today, we will often see the world where we live hate us for Jesus' sake. We spoke in earlier chapters on how Satan pretty well has the world in chaos and complete blindness to God's will for the inhabitants of earth. The Gospel of John chapter 1 speaks on this issue. Jesus Christ is the light. John 1:5, 10 explain the darkness not comprehending the light, and the world not knowing Him. The world was full of sin, death, and darkness before Jesus Christ took the form of man and became the sacrifice for man to receive that light in our hearts. Without Jesus Christ, we cannot come to the light and salvation of God. Our souls before knowing Jesus Christ as our Lord and Savior are in darkness—darkness inhabited with sin, captivity, remorse, lies, deceit, and fear. Once we receive Jesus into our hearts and begin a new life in Him, the light begins to chase away the dark. Those remaining around us who have not received the light of Christ will not comprehend our transformation. Regrettably, most of this world does not comprehend that light.

The verse in 2 Timothy 3:12 is telling us that as a receiver of that beautiful light of Christ, be prepared for the persecutions of this world. Jesus tells us in Matthew chapter 5 that we are blessed and should rejoice when the world persecutes us for His sake. Let's be honest, it is hard to be joyful when we are being persecuted. Why would Jesus tell us such a thing? Surely God knows that it goes against all human nature to be positive and happy when under attack or when we feel like the outsider looking in. Jesus tells us this for the spiritual nature, not the human nature. When we are being criticized for our Christian life, then we are obviously giving the example of a Christian life that others clearly see.

Others who live for the world and the treasures thereof, will feel threatened or superior to a Christian life. People can be very defensive towards what they do not understand. I will again use myself as an example. An example I am not at all proud of, but I feel I must be honest so others can one day be honest as well. I am not proud of this, but I am forgiven.

Before giving my life to Jesus Christ, I was a huge critic of anyone who had. I really viewed this as an excuse for a person to give up in life and cease to deal with reality. I believed people had become so unwilling to fight for their own beliefs that they took the easy way out. I viewed them as people who must have been guilty of horrible things, and they realized their only hope to ever be forgiven was to start proclaiming Jesus. I viewed these people as weak and often pathetic.

Like I said, I am not at all proud of this view I had lived under before knowing Christ. I will tell you, however, as I am writing this I cannot help but to laugh at myself and be amazed by how God used His wisdom to deal with me. My views were exactly right in most cases, but completely misunderstood in my heart. I was right, most people had no way out and finally gave up and gave their life to Jesus. I had no way out of the misery and anxiety I was experiencing in the days leading up to surrendering to Christ. I had no fight left in me whatsoever. I had done horrible things and was guilty of great pain inflicted upon others. I had become one of those weak and pathetic souls I used to persecute. Thank God I was one of those people! The perceptions in my mind, the lies of Satan he has the world in bondage to, all fight against us to the very moment of surrender to Christ. Once we have surrendered, the perceptions in our minds begin changing, but those in the world who do not know Christ remain the same. This transformation God is performing through you should become a major contrast to the world that Satan is in command of.

As this contrast becomes more apparent, expect the persecutions to increase. Friends who could always rely upon us to help out with an inappropriate good time will see we no longer partake in things we once did. This will leave them confused and angry. They will believe we are turning our backs on them or think we are too good for them now that we're such holy rollers. Coworkers who were used to our filthy mouths we once knew will be baffled at the fact we do not talk that way as much, and hopefully one day, not at all. There will be extreme opposition by any and all groups of people with the *anything goes* attitude that so much of this world shares. We will be seen as insensitive, unapproachable, and uncivilized. God gives us very clear dos and don'ts in the Bible. We will live this life for others to see and others who do not wish to follow the don'ts will not like the fact that we are. Then, there are persecutions from the areas we don't expect. Family members who are not saved will be unable to grasp this new found hope we have. They may accuse us of being false or putting on an act out of desperation. I can assure the husbands who read this book, a wife that has seen year-after-year of a selfish husband, probably won't sing for joy the moment we tell them of our salvation. Our nearest loved ones may even unknowingly be one of our main areas of persecution in the beginning. Be patient, it will pass with time. Simply stay surrendered and see the final outcome through faith, not today's catastrophe.

Those were examples of what fellow brothers and sisters can do in the area of persecution. We must not underestimate that Satan will be persecuting us as well. Satan will come after us with all he has. We may suffer the loss of job, finances, and possessions. We may be placed in positions with non-Christians who may attack us on a daily basis. Satan will work endlessly to penetrate our mind with doubts and regrets. Satan has alcohol, drugs, sex, greed, pride, and vanity to lure people into performing his work. Satan believes, if the cost be too high for us to remain faithful we will cash it all-in and return to his forces, along with the world we once knew. *Satan is a liar!* He does not wish to give us eternal life in paradise. In order to see that eternity of being in the presence of God, we must identify the persecutions of this short life will pass. At one time in my life, I could only see a few years down the road. I only prioritized those that would bring me gain in this world. Surrendering my life to Jesus Christ has made me a visionary. I now see the future eternity God has promised me. This life will pass and all we know of this world will perish. Jesus Christ is preparing a mansion for us in the kingdom of heaven—that mansion will remain forever.

Hebrews 11:13-16 talks about strangers and pilgrims. These verses speak of confession, witness, and testimony of faithful elect of God who seek a country built through foundational truths and Heavenly principles. This is unattainable with: true friendship with the world, longing for acceptance of the world, and fear of being left out of what the world offers us. This country is not existent in this present world of which we are a part. The lie we have all too often fell victim to was that we could possibly attain our heart's desires and peace through anything the world offers.

Our time upon the earth is short, but our selfish demands and fears of our flesh are great.

Our heavenly Father knew we would struggle with this. His hopes for our victory are why He sacrificed His Son in order to ensure our inheritance with Him in the country we truly seek. But we must identify that, first, our longing for peace and security cannot be sufficed by this world. Secondly, our only possible way to overcome the flesh is through the spirit of Christ. Third, through growing faith, further crucify our flesh which continually struggles to return us back to the country we have left behind.

I love the phrase more and more "burn the ships." I am learning with each day that the ship which brought us to where God has called and chosen us could return us to the country we knew before knowing Jesus Christ. The ship is truly constructed out of physical and spiritual materials that can quietly sneak back up and reconstruct a vessel prepared to launch across the ocean of salvation with the destination of worldly treasures on the horizon! We are the builders of the ship…any remaining parts that remain washed up on the beach of faith we have encountered will continue to move in and out with the tides of trials and unexpected persecutions of this world and life. They will bang against our shores with the haunting memory of the wreck, which led us to our first arrival.

Only faith of the inheritance, which lies ahead when we spiritually view the terrain, can keep us from humanely looking back across the ocean where we may have once seemed assured and grounded in our worldly inhabitants. If we stare too long across the ocean, we may begin to gather some of the rubble together once again and begin building our ships with the unknowing preparation of setting across the ocean to a more comfortable, accepted, and successful fellowship with the world. We begin by building a hull from any leftover pieces of selfishness lying upon the beach. Then some nice thick sections of fear make a great stem for cutting through any difficult moral issues which could arise in the form of waves to stop our ship from sailing. Pride and foolishness are a wonderful combination for a solid stern and fitting last image for those remaining on the beach we are leaving to view as we sail into the abyss. And of course let's not forget our sails and mast that are driven by disbelief, lack of patience, and immediate need for personal gratification!

When our vessel of destruction first hits the beach of salvation, we need to get out and set fire to the ship immediately! Sometimes we get worried about the rough terrain the spiritual world holds in store and we run to extinguish the flames coming from our ships in hopes to leave an escape route if needed. Then again, even when the main body of the ship has been burned, some smaller pieces may have been washed to shore and buried under the sand at first. These are not noticed at the start, but will eventually surface and then show life in the country we have left and willingness to be reconstructed if their owner will submit to working with them. We need to understand a small fire is necessary at this time. Perhaps the big fire took care of the main vessel, but little fires cannot be overlooked when needed! If we don't burn the ship and all remaining remnants when surfaced, how can we ever truly eliminate our return to the world and confess our relentless pursuit of our Lord!

Only then can we say: "I am a stranger and pilgrim to this earth." My country is yet to come, but some remnants which cannot be burned remain within me in the form of the true living God! That is the vessel I will dedicate my spiritual life to reconstructing. And I will pray the Father will at all time be my master builder!

I will not tell you that I am overcome with joy during persecutions and trials. Oftentimes through my own pain and stubbornness, God reveals yet another lesson for me to learn that brings me closer to Jesus, my Savior. I will merely tell you to look upon the example Jesus Christ gave us. Jesus underwent more persecution than any of us will ever imagine. Jesus was arrested, beaten, scourged, and crucified. We do not understand persecution such as what our Lord went through. Through it all, He remained surrendered and obedient to God. There are parts of this world where being a Christian can bring persecution that will cost the believer their life. This loss of life is tragic and wrong, but look upon the example these saints are leaving for us. I can hear their spirits talking to us all. I will stand for my belief in Jesus Christ my Lord. He stood for me!

In John 14:18 Jesus tells us, "I will not leave you orphans; I will come to you" In John 16:33 Jesus tells us, "These things I have spoken to you, that in Me you may have peace. In the world you will have tribulation; but be of good cheer, I have overcome the world." In Revelation 3:10 Jesus tells us, "Because you have kept My command to persevere, I also will keep you from the hour of trial that shall come upon the whole world, to test those who dwell on the earth."

Once surrendered, believed, and lived, we are becoming a soldier for Jesus Christ. Persecutions will come from many diverse places, along with those who dwell in darkness and from Satan as well. If there be any reason to feel blessed and rejoice, I believe it to be the following: living for Jesus Christ and His teachings has placed us in position to suffer as our Lord had to suffer. How better to know we are on the path of righteousness as to suffer for a time for the one who suffered for all. Jesus is telling us to rejoice in the spirit, we are on the right path to spend eternity with Him!

## Warning for Unbelief

> Beware, brethren, lest there be in any of you an evil heart of unbelief in departing from the living God.
>
> —Hebrews 3:12

As we approach the end phase of "Live" in *3:12 Transformation,* God reminds us to remain faithful, believe in our hearts, and be completely on fire for Christ. Hebrews 3:12 is a warning to us that we could fall out of grace and return to our past if our hearts do not remain believing. Hebrews speaks how God worked through Moses to lead His people out of Egypt and how the people, once again, hardened their hearts. They failed to see and believe all God had done for them. As a result of their disbelieving hearts, Israel spent forty years wandering in the desert. "So I swore in My wrath, 'They shall not enter My rest" (Hebrews 3:11).

How could the people of Israel turn away from God? God freed them from bondage, parted the Red Sea for their escape and destruction of their enemy, provided food and water for them, and guided their path with His presence. How could people's hearts be hardened after such salvation by God Himself? The answer is unbelief. As earlier stated in this book, I hold fast to belief being our biggest success or failure along the way of our transformation. How does belief affect the way we live? We will live the way we believe. If we feel in our hearts that an action would be wrong in the sight of God, and we choose not to act upon it as a result, we are living by God's presence in faith. If we choose to do things that go against God but do not believe any consequences will come, or just don't care, we have hardened our hearts to the Lord.

I was forgiven for all my sins and led from the bondage of sin and addictions. I have never gone without food, clothing, and shelter. God has given me a vision and a work to perform for His kingdom to be spread, and His Son to be glorified. In my experience, God has reunited my family, marriage, and placed peace and joy in my heart I'd never imagined. God has been so gracious and merciful. Could I ever become hardened and unbelieving? Could you? The answer is yes, on both counts. All we do needs to be done with gratefulness and remembrance of what God has done for us. God needs to be our first love. As soon as priorities change in our lives, our relationship with God will change as well. God has to be the number one priority. Number one before wives, husbands, work, children, money, sports, etc. If we only call upon God when we need Him, I believe God will feel like He is no longer our priority and first love. If we thank God for the miracle but then go about living life selfishly and how we choose, we will hear the words from Jesus one day, "I never knew you" (Matt. 7:23).

This departing from God sounds like it would be a huge decision. We would have to be consciously involved in such a decision which affected our lives, right? Not at all! This departing from our Lord is usually subtle and in the form of baby steps. We slowly begin consulting less with God in prayer and worship. We give too much time to our thoughts and plans rather than seeking God's plan for us. We become more believing in our ability and resources and less seeking of God's. These signs, in early stages, do not set off an alarm that notifies fellow Christians: alarms with screaming high pitches alerting the need of spiritual counsel and accountability. These are signs which our minds need to see early. If we fail to see the signs or choose to ignore them, our heart becomes a partaker in turning away from God as well. Then we will reach a stage where our fellow brothers and sisters also clearly see our signs of disbelief. Our actions will reflect what our heart and mind are being consumed with. We will be departing from the Living God through disbelief once again!

Our intimate relationship with God is on the line if we do not strangle any oxygen from the neck of disbelief as soon as it gasps for air. Seek guidance from God daily. Today, if you hear His voice, harden not your hearts.

> For we have become partakers of Christ if we hold the beginning of our confidence steadfast to the end.
>
> Hebrews 3:14

## All-in for Jesus

> Can a fig tree, my brethren, bear olives, or a grapevine bear figs? Thus no spring yields both salt water and fresh.
>
> —James 3:12

Our confidence began when we accepted Jesus Christ into our hearts. We asked Him into our hearts with brokenness, humility, hope, faith, and longing for His presence to guide us. If we stand fast with that desire in our life every day and live that example, we will not harden our hearts.

James 3:12 is further reinforcing the all-in for Jesus Christ lifestyle we need to live. Can a spring yield both fresh and saltwater? Our souls are a spring for God. These springs should flow with freshwater that will sustain ourselves and give refreshments to others for the Lord. Our spring can also bring forth saltwater if we choose to live a life of sin. Saltwater will overtake any freshwater in our stream and try to contaminate the water of others as well. In John 7:38, Jesus tells us, "He who believes in Me, as the Scripture has said, out of his heart will flow rivers of living water." When we seek the Lord's guidance, our spring is flowing with the direction of the Holy Spirit. Living waters come from Jesus Christ. Our waters from Christ will refresh us when thirsty and quench us when dry. If our springs be of salt and sin, we cannot maintain life in Christ. Our waters will lead to our death and give no refreshment to ourselves or those around us.

Chapter 3 of James also speaks of our tongues which we can use to proclaim our Lord, or profane our Lord. We can bless our fellow brothers and sisters with our words or murder them with our words. Our tongue is so small, yet we use it as if it is larger than God. Cease the attacking of one another! Hateful and cruel words are launched in attacks to destroy each other's joy, cause fear, promote anger, and cause dissension. These are shameful words of death used to further kill the hopes, dreams, and beliefs of others. Our belittling of others can cause laughter among our peers. Our filthy words focusing on vulgarity and profanity are confession of our giving into lust and wicked thoughts. Jesus tells us to give praise and thanks to our Father. Witness to others what God has done with encouragement and love. Bless others with prayers to God. Let God's word flow from your tongue. Use your God given gift of speech to give God's good news to others!

Our lives need to be lived by this example. We are believers in Jesus Christ and will consistently follow His teachings in life. We are no longer in the utterly broken stage when we first accepted Jesus into our hearts. If so, we can expect some salt to mix into the freshwater at times. But once surrendered, believing and living a life for Christ, there has to be zealousness in our heart for Jesus. Hold yourself to a higher standard in Jesus. Expect to be that spring that can give another soul the thirst-quenching witnessing needed at the time. Live for Jesus, by Jesus, and according to Jesus. Give all you have for God each day! Do not compromise that which God has spoken to you! Surrender, believe, and live what Jesus Christ has done and the life He sets for us to live. Then, we are ready to take the next phase of 3:12 Transformation—the area of our life that Jesus Christ gave His life for, so all could hear the good news!

## LIVE

*3:12 Transformation*

Do you believe God has an individual calling and purpose which only you can perform?

________________________________________

________________________________________

________________________________________

________________________________________

In what areas do you feel your foundation in Christ is strong?

________________________________________

________________________________________

________________________________________

________________________________________

Explain love without Jesus in your life. Explain love with Jesus in your life.

What could be warning signs that you are departing from God?

Explain your current role(s) you hold and how you can *Live* as Jesus has taught you.

What is your willingness to be all in for Jesus at this time? What does it require?

PROCLAIM
LIVE
BELIEVE
SURRENDER

# PROCLAIM

## Proclaim God's Faithfulness

> So He said, "I will certainly be with you. And this shall be a sign to you that I have sent you: When you have brought the people out of Egypt, you shall serve God on this mountain."
>
> —Exodus 3:12

Now, we are entering into service for the Lord! Proclaim the good news of salvation! Jesus Christ died, was buried, and rose again. After Christ's resurrection He ascended to the Father. We who believe become the example of Christ on earth after that point. Those who have been given mercy will give mercy. Those who have been set free will freely give to others. Those who know Christ will introduce Him to those who do not.

The first verse of "Proclaim" is Exodus 3:12. In chapter 3 of Exodus, God is speaking to Moses through a burning bush. God tells Moses how He has seen the oppression of His people in Egypt and plans to deliver them out of captivity. God informs Moses that Moses will go to Egypt and be the one God has chosen to lead the Israelites out of Egypt. In Exodus 3:12, Moses is reassured that God will be present with him. God gives Moses a sign for the future that will manifest itself once Moses has followed God's word. God is sending Moses into Egypt to proclaim the freedom and liberty of God's people. Moses is to proclaim this to the Israelites, all the people of Egypt, and Pharaoh the king. In chapter 4 of Exodus, Moses doubted, questioned, and asked God to choose someone else. Moses had to surrender to God's will, believe God would be with Him, and live and perform as God showed him; then, he was able to proclaim to God's people freedom from oppression.

We all have similar stages to go through as Moses did. All our efforts and learning to walk as Christ has shown us is leading to this point. "For you were bought at a price; therefore glorify God in your body and in your spirit, which are God's" (1 Corinthians 6:20). The purchase price was the blood of Jesus Christ. The purchase that we all receive through faith is salvation in Christ. The price for us is to proclaim that purchase to others for the glory of God. In Exodus 3:12, what God is telling us in my words is as follows: "Go forth and spread the message of salvation. I will be with you. You will lead others to freedom, and they shall worship My name. I will show you My faithfulness."

When God first gave me the vision of 3:12 Transformation through the dream I received, I was excited and hopeful. I took this to my pastor within a few days and shared it with him. Some time was spent praying for God's guidance, researching the verses, and weighing the options on beginning a group at our church according to this vision and message. After three to four months, my pastor and I met again. I had developed some paperwork and a rough outline for the program. Pastor asked me again to pray on the matter and also gave me some other information pertaining to other options for existing recovery groups. Our church had been seeking a recovery program for some time but was waiting for the right one and a willing volunteer to commit to it. My pastor asked me to look over the other programs, look over 3:12 Transformation, and decide which program to start at our church. He also gave me complete support and said he would trust my decision. I had received the vision months earlier and was confident while preparing all God had been leading me with. All of a sudden, when faced with the decision of 3:12 Transformation or another existing group, I seemed to doubt for a short time.

I felt a sense of fear that no one would listen to me. I realized beginning a new recovery program, whether based solely on Jesus Christ or not, was near impossible with all the existing programs that already had a following and the name established. I worried my church, pastor, and I would be made to look like fools when the program crashed and burned. With a broken heart, I had myself talked into not risking it, and going with an existing spiritually-based recovery program. After all, I wanted to help others find hope. It didn't matter whether or not it was my program; it only had to be God's program. I decided to look at the chapter 3s and verse 12s once again. I was trying to find peace on the issue. I prayed to God and asked for His guidance and my acceptance no matter what His will was. Originally, 3:12 Transformation had fifteen verses. There were certain verses I did not see at first, or did not feel they related to recovery. After the prayer to God for direction and guidance, I sat down once again and opened the Bible. I was going to go through all sixty six books of the Bible again and was determined to make my decision. God gave me the answer, confirmation, and calling my spirit was longing to hear!

In the second book of the Bible, Exodus 3:12 came to life to me. This was one of the verses I didn't see as pertaining to recovery originally. God used this verse to be my burning bush. It was time to truly see God's calling in my life. The calling was to proclaim God's message to others! Fear of failure vanished. Questioning how I'd be received by others was no longer a thought. The promise God gives that people in bondage would be freed, and they would come to worship Him. I faithfully believed with all my heart! God launched me into proclamation at this point. There was no turning back after that day. I went to my pastor with boldness and confidence that 3:12 Transformation was the program for our church. I became willing to lead others and put my reputation and story out in the public for the world to see, regardless of the outcome.

How do I explain my time of doubt? I have come to believe that period of time was needed in my journey with the Lord. I believe God wanted to see my desire to serve Him exclusively, and the importance that this placed upon my soul. God wanted to see me exhaust my human thought process so He could show me His message. It was a faith builder and promise God wanted me to see at that very time in my life. God wants us to proclaim what we have been recipients of. God will show each and every one of us our calling and the perfect time to proclaim that calling. Once we receive that confirmation from the Lord, we will proclaim with boldness and confidence our hopes turned into faith and true belief!

## Boldly Proclaim New Hope to Others

> Therefore, since we have such hope, we use great boldness of speech.
>
> 2 Corinthians 3:12

The verse in 2 Corinthians 3:12 tells us to boldly proclaim new hope to others. That is exactly what we are to do—spread hope and good news. Proclaim to others how they can receive the same peace, joy, and salvation you have come to know by knowing Jesus Christ.

> The Spirit of the Lord God is upon Me, because the Lord has anointed Me to preach good tidings to the poor; He has sent Me to heal the brokenhearted, to proclaim liberty to the captives, and the opening of the prison to those who are bound.
>
> Isaiah 61: 1

This verse in Isaiah is a prophecy of the words that would be spoken by Christ the Messiah. Jesus Christ fulfills this prophecy in Luke 4:17–21. We are the ones to carry this message and continue representing Christ in this day and age. Through our testimony, we are given power through the Holy Spirit to relay this message. We are commissioned by God to preach the gospel, heal the brokenhearted, proclaim liberty to the captives, and free those oppressed. Jesus Christ is alive—Jesus was, is, and always will be. We have become the disciples of Christ and are now responsible to proclaim salvation to the broken and lost. When we go out and witness to others, do it with conviction and belief of what you have experienced. Put passion and love in your heart when proclaiming Jesus. We have been freed and given God's anointing to carry on the work of Christ. How many brothers and sisters will we give hope to if we sound unsure and complacent? Now, I realize this will be a process. Actively pray to God and the Holy Spirit to increase your proclaiming and boldness in Christ. Trust what God has shown you thus far. Your proclaiming is God's glorification. God will guide you.

The apostles of Jesus Christ give us a true example of transformation and boldness we can all take comfort in. On the night Jesus was betrayed, all the apostles abandoned Him. They ran away into hiding to protect themselves. Peter denied Jesus three times the night He was arrested and taken into custody. I can only imagine the utter fear and anxiety the apostles must have undergone. The shame and guilt of their betrayal of Christ, which they must have been subject to, could have been nothing less than overbearing upon their spirits. The man they knew to be the Son of God, whom all their hopes and beliefs were given to, was taken from them and condemned in a single night. The next day they would have heard all the reports of how their Master had been beaten, scourged, ridiculed, and mocked. Then they would be told that Jesus was crucified and He died upon the cross. He was taken down and laid in a tomb, and a stone was rolled in front of it. It would have been hard not to give up at this time in their life; ashamed, guilt ridden, broken, and scared. Life would have seemed useless to continue at this time in the apostles' lives. What good could possibly come of such tragic events?

Jesus rose from the grave three days later! In God's wonderful, mysterious way, the first recorded transformations of broken people had begun. The apostles were forgiven. They saw, firsthand, God's gift of grace through Jesus Christ. The chains of bondage which held the apostles from going forward boldly had been shattered. Their darkness was turned into light. Salvation had come to the followers of Christ! The world attempted to kill Jesus Christ and place Him in the grave for eternity. But Jesus Christ conquered the grave for all His followers to spend eternity with Him!

Forty days later Jesus Christ ascended into heaven with the Father. He instructed His apostles to remain in Jerusalem and wait for His promise. He promised to send His Holy Spirit to them.

> "But you shall receive power when the Holy Spirit has come upon you: and you shall be witnesses to Me in Jerusalem, and in all Judea and Samaria, and to the end of the earth."
>
> Acts 1:8

When the apostles received the Holy Spirit as promised, there was a dramatic transformation in their lives. These once broken men who ran away from the Lord were now given power and boldness. They were given wisdom and faith. They were given the words to proclaim and testify of Jesus Christ and witness what had taken place in their lives. Peter, who had denied Christ three times, stood up on the day of Pentecost and boldly proclaimed Jesus Christ! As a result of Peter's transformation and power through the Holy Spirit, his proclaiming Jesus Christ led 3,000 souls to repentance and belief in Jesus that same day!

Other apostles went on to write Gospels contained in the Bible (John, Matthew). The apostles proclaimed the good news of Jesus Christ throughout the region. By their testimonies, others carried the message of Christ and salvation also. Then others became partakers in the proclaiming. As a result, the apostles of Jesus, once seemingly lost and without guidance, turned the world upside down through the Holy Spirit of God. The Holy Spirit which revealed to them how to proclaim boldly the new hope and life they had been given!

> But the anointing which you have received from Him abides in you, and you do not need that anyone teach you; but as the same anointing teaches you concerning all things, and is true, and is not a lie, and just as it has taught you, you will abide in Him.
>
> 1 John 2:27

God's Holy Spirit will be your teacher. You may be led to others for God's word and guidance as well. Just believe that God will give you the boldness, confidence, and words to proclaim and magnify His holy name!

## Proclaim God's Blessings for the Faithful

> For the eyes of the Lord are on the righteous, and His ears are open to their prayers; but the face of the Lord is against those who do evil.
>
> —1 Peter 3:12

The verse in 1 Peter 3:12 is telling us to proclaim the fact that God hears the prayers and pleas of His people. If we are living a life modeled after Jesus Christ's example then we are seeking that righteousness Peter is speaking of. We have seen in the last chapter and throughout this book how God will be with us. God will bless us and be faithful to our requests when given to Him from a pure heart and for His glory. God will have His hand upon us, shelter us, and be receptive to our needs and prayer. Proclaim this intimacy to others. Encourage and lift others up during their times of doubt and questioning. Assure them that God's Spirit is present with them and will give them peace if sought.

In Genesis 9:9, Noah was obedient to God and followed the calling God had given him. As a result, God tells Noah, "And as for Me, behold, I establish My covenant with you and with your descendants after you." God says after Israel has repented for their transgressions, God will establish a new covenant with them.

> "But this is the covenant that I will make with the house of Israel after those days, says the Lord: I will put My law in their minds, and write it on their hearts; and I will be their God, and they shall be My people"
>
> Jeremiah 31:33

In these two verses, God is telling us of covenants He will make to His people. Jeremiah points to the new covenant through Jesus Christ and repentance for past sins. Genesis tells us of God establishing a covenant with us after obedience. We have made the repentance for our past sins through our belief and confession in Jesus Christ—God's new covenant. We have surrendered, believed, and lived as God has instructed. Throughout this transformation, God has placed His law in our minds and written it in our hearts. We are partakers of this covenant with God! We are the people of the almighty God! Chosen, forgiven, freed, and anointed to proclaim this salvation! God will not turn His back on His people. God will not break His covenant. God is faithful to His people. Proclaim this faithfulness!

The verse in 1 Peter 3:12 also tells us, we are to proclaim God's anger toward those who turn away from God. This is somewhat of a tricky area. There is a lot of human error that can occur when pointing out someone's faults. We can do this with confidence and love. It is possible to convict fellow brothers and sisters' hearts without condemning their soul. We can share our testimony to all those who will listen. If we see a brother struggling, we can relate to them through conversation on how we struggled as well and what we found to deliver us. When there are circumstances that cause us to distance ourselves from others, we often are asked to explain ourselves. We are given an opportunity to share our testimony and faith with them. The choice is theirs on whether or not they hear the testimony. We are obedient and have done our part when we give it.

During these opportunities, be sure to stress the life of bondage you knew, compared to the sense of freedom you now enjoy. As a proclaimer for Christ, we must act upon these opportunities. Do not be ashamed of the gospel. If we are, our Lord will also be ashamed of us. Pray for true ability through the Holy Spirit to let us see the heart of those still suffering and struggling. We as Christians are seeking further souls to share the kingdom of heaven with our Lord. If we only proclaim to those who are saved, how do we accomplish helping others know Jesus Christ. The verse in 2 Timothy 3:12 will come into play again when proclaiming to the lost. There's no doubt, we will suffer persecutions during these times. There will also be times when some hear our testimony and give their lives to Jesus Christ. No matter what the immediate case will be, remember God has a covenant with you! He is not going anywhere!

## Proclaim the Return of the King

> Looking for and hastening the coming of the day of God, because of which the heavens will be dissolved, being on fire, and the elements will melt with fervent heat? Nevertheless we, according to His promise, look for new heavens and a new earth in which righteousness dwells.
>
> —2 Peter 3:12–13

In 2 Peter 3:12, we are being led to proclaim that all we know on earth will be dissolved and Jesus Christ, King of kings, will return. Peter tells us in this chapter that the day of the Lord will indeed come and will come as a thief in the night. The world as we know it at this present time will no longer exist. All will be made new. Are we to stand on the corners of our cities with signs that read "The end is near, repent"? My heart is not leading me that way. I believe, we are to proclaim God's beautiful promise of eternity with Him. There will be new heavens and a new earth where righteousness dwells. If righteousness dwells upon the coming heavens and earth, who will be dwelling there? Obviously, the righteous will be the inhabitants, not those who think they are righteous. Proclaim Christ's return when He will call His righteous home with Him. 2 Peter 3:12 coincides with 1 Peter perfectly on the topic of "Proclaim." Both verses are telling us to remain faithful to God and proclaim His promises to His people. We also see in both verses the need to proclaim to those not living as God has taught and the longing God has for them to join Him. The Bible tells us that God is not willing that any should perish but all should come to repentance (2 Peter 3:9).

We should reflect the same attitude in our proclaiming as God has. The more we witness of Jesus Christ, the more we share our story of transformation, the more hope we spread to those yet to know of God's mercy and love. Also, we need to hold fellow Christians accountable, as well as ourselves. Remind each other that God is in control. Stand shoulder to shoulder with one another and further strengthen each other in Christ.

Another theme which is very popular and gaining steam in the world today is the question: "How can a loving God allow all the evil in the world and let innocent people get hurt?" "How can God allow innocent children to be assaulted?"

These questions are exactly why we need to put 1 and 2 Peter 3:12 into action through our faith and proclaiming. God will not allow all the wickedness to take place. God is a loving God and will bring an end to this madness ran amok by the wicked world in which we live. I believe it is only due to God's great love for us that He is holding off His return. God is allowing us to choose repentance through His Son and have salvation. The Bible clearly states God's disapproval of the wicked actions of mankind in the book of Revelation. Jesus Christ will return and bring an end to all this chaos and tragedy. Jesus will bring an end to all the misery that much of the world is blaming on God's non-existence and lack of love. This day will come. If we are not seeking righteousness through Jesus Christ, we will not be inhabitants of the new world in which our Loving God shall provide us.

We have been given rebirth. Many in the world are still in bondage and sin. We must stay focused on God's calling and Jesus' teachings to remain in the truth. God's word and agenda is what we are to follow. The world has many people amongst us spreading false doctrine, false hope, and promoting sinful lifestyles for their own gain. God will honor His righteous people. Proclaim that honor and faith we have in God. Witness and guide those in need of the truth. Take upon yourself this responsibility God has given you. The responsibility will not be one of burden, rather one of joy and peace. Jesus Christ Himself gave us instruction on how to proclaim.

> "Go into all the world and preach the gospel to every creature. He who believes and is baptized will be saved; he who does not believe will be condemned."
>
> Mark 15:15–16

This is all our calling to share. Come and be made free and new with Jesus Christ. Believe in His holy name. Your eternity is dependent upon it!

## Proclaim the Promise of Jesus Christ!

> He who overcomes, I will make him a pillar in the temple of My God, and he shall go out no more. I will write on him the name of My God and the name of the city of My God, the New Jerusalem, which comes down out of heaven from My God. And I will write on him My new name.
>
> —Revelation 3:12

The final verse in 3:12 Transformation is quite a promise from our Lord, Jesus Christ. Jesus has a lot of plans for us. This chapter will focus on the proclaiming to others the promise, but I want you to personally proclaim this promise to yourself as well. This verse represents Jesus speaking to the Apostle John, the writer of the book of Revelation. Jesus is addressing the seven churches. Jesus is telling those in the church to persevere, have faith, and stand true in His teachings. He then speaks what we read in Revelation 3:12. He is speaking to those who overcome the lies and tribulations of this world; and, those who will repent for their sinful life and overcome the world they have known by their faith in Jesus Christ. Jesus is telling how He will claim those overcomers. He will write His name upon them. He will write on them the name of His God and the name of the city of His God—the new Jerusalem. Jesus is taking one hundred percent ownership of those who overcome. He is going to reward them with paradise, peace, joy, and His presence forever.

We are those overcomers. We are the ones Jesus Christ is claiming. All the promises that are written are for you and me to share together with Christ, our Lord! Our overcoming is made simple when we surrender to Jesus Christ and let Him bear our burdens that once overcame us. We truly and merely need to overcome ourselves and this world. It can be done through the blood of Jesus Christ, but not on our own. Jesus is pleading with us to overcome our fears, worries, selfishness, pain and struggles, and give them to Him with faith! God loves us so much more than words can say. Why else would He have created us, give us chance after chance, sacrifice His Son for us, and then given one encouragement after another throughout the scriptures for us to have in this life for spiritual guidance?

God goes as far as telling us we have overcome. "For whatever is born of God overcomes the world" (1 John 5:4). And this is the victory that has overcome the world—our faith.

There is the faith key again. Our faith—our belief, is what enables our victory in Christ and over this world. Through our faith we overcome! Proclaim your faith for all to know! Proclaim your faith for the world to know! Shout with your spirit, "I am an overcomer in Christ." Proclaim this to yourself and believe it! God cannot lie.

God tells us the overcomers will be the victors, and the wicked will not defeat us. Do not hate the wicked and the lifestyle they lead that at times, seems like they will never be held accountable for. God tells us "These will make war with the Lamb, and the Lamb will overcome them, for He is Lord of lords and King of Kings; and those who are with Him are called, chosen, and faithful"(Revelation 17:14). Proclaim our future victory with Christ to yourself and all those who hear you. Witness to others in faith and hope that they can join the winning side of Jesus Christ.

What does it mean to you that you have overcome and will go out no more? To me, it makes all the difference for my surrender, belief, and life I will live. When I contemplate the reality that Jesus Christ Himself is telling me, "He shall go out no more."(Rev. 3:12), it takes it to a spiritual level that words seem inadequate for. The feelings of worthlessness will not return. The doubt of eternity and what it involves is gone. The urgency of claiming victory in the human race is no longer important. My marriage will not be threatened by my selfish actions again. My family will come to know Jesus Christ and live their lives for Him when their time with God becomes known. I will go out no more. I will not turn my back on my God. I am told I will be made a pillar in the temple of God.

A pillar is a structure of strength that supports another structure. The structure we are being made to support is the temple of God, not a simple building by this world's standard. As soon as we surrender and give our lives to Jesus, the pillar we are to become begins a molding process through the blood of Christ. This pillar will be made from materials of faith and obedience. It will be cast and cured to stand the test of time for the eternal kingdom of God. On earth, our pillars will support the church of Jesus Christ, which will extend into heaven, for God to take pleasure upon. What does overcome say to you? What does "Go out no more" mean to you? What does being made a pillar mean to you? It needs to mean everything, and most of all, you need to believe!

> He who overcomes shall inherit all things, and I will be His God and he shall be My son.
>
> Revelation 21:7

God wants to give you all things. It makes all the little things we chased in life seem pretty futile, doesn't it? We are sons and daughters of God. Our Father wants to give us inheritance to share with Jesus Christ. Proclaim this beautiful promise. Where do you turn from here if you do not accept? Once knowing the peace and presence of God, can you turn away? Where would you go? What would you do? Who will fight your battles, the ones you cannot win? Who will sacrifice their life for you? We all like to be the winner in life. Nobody wishes to be on the losing team. If you are reading this book and do not know Jesus Christ as your personal Lord and Savior, ask Him to become that now. You do not want to risk another day, another year, or another ten years. Jesus Christ will come as a thief in the night upon His return. Please don't be caught on the losing team. Give your life to Jesus. Be an overcomer and win!

For those of us who have given our life to Christ, I challenge all of us to look at the life we are leading for Him. Are we doing everything we can for the spread of the kingdom of God? Have we become so comfortable with our own salvation that the salvation of our brothers and sisters is no longer a priority? Are we proclaiming Jesus Christ and the gift He has given us? Have we become lukewarm in our walk with Christ? We can all do more, give more, and believe more! It is our responsibility to unite all the denominations of Christianity as one unified church in the name of Jesus Christ, our Lord. As pillars of the temple of God, we must perform the following steps:

1. Surrender our prides and unproductive rivalries from amongst each other.
2. Believe we are all fellow brothers and sisters in Christ, called as a whole for His glory.
3. Live a life that exemplifies to others the need to join us in living for Christ; and, live by God's word, not by our compromises.
4. Proclaim the peace and beauty a life in Christ will lead to by our testimonies!

## Proclaim

### *3:12 Transformation*

How would you proclaim your transformation to others using Surrender, Believe & Live as your outline?

How does hope and confidence in Christ affect your proclaiming to others?

How do you believe you can best proclaim to non-believers? Those not strong in their faith?

What does Revelation 3:12 say to you?

## Closing Thoughts and Prayers

I want to encourage all of you. It makes no difference if we are new Christians or lifelong followers of Christ. We all play a role in God's direction for this earth we live upon. I believe God is calling His people to return to Him and make ready for the future events that will take place. God is giving mercy and blessings to those willing and seeking to receive them. The divisional lines are being clearly drawn in the world. You either live for God, or you are chasing evil through the short-term gains of living for the world. I believe God's Holy Spirit is descending upon the earth at this time in history for those who will be saved to recognize and be given strength through faith. I also believe this solely be for the purpose of saving as many souls as possible for God's will and great love He has for all. God's Holy Spirit will ripple across this earth for all to know. For those who believe, it will be a rushing tidal wave of truth that convicts their soul.

> Father, please let Your people come to You completely with an open and humble heart. Let us know Your great wisdom, peace, mercies, and love. Lord, through Your Son, Jesus Christ, may we follow the guidance You have given us. May our souls be set ablaze for Your glory and magnification Lord. Search our hearts and our minds and remove anything that offends You Father. Give us the strength needed to trust in Your holiness and peace of mind in knowing You are our provider. Father, rise

up your church through Your Holy Spirit to become what Jesus Christ, our Lord sacrificed Himself for it to be, according to Your infinite wisdom. And Father, give us courage to sacrifice our fears, so others may know You as well. By the power of Your Son, Jesus Christ we ask this of You Father, Amen!

When first developing 3:12 Transformation, I felt the desire to capture what I believed it truly expressed, so that anyone could understand the program fairly easily and quickly. As a result, God revealed to me a poem that contains fifteen verses from the program. I have added it into the ending of this book, with the hopes it will read as God's message to you individually, as it did to me.

May you desire to know God more each day!

## 3:12 Transformation Poem

My child,
I will be with you, do not be afraid
I will show others, the commitment which we've made (Exodus 3:12)
For My child I dearly love you, I'll correct your evil ways
And you will sense My Spirit, each and every day (Proverbs/ Ezekiel 3:12)
I will remove your foolish pride, and the doubts of your soul

And fill it with humility, till it overflows (Zephaniah 3:12)
My child, believe these words, I am telling you
And enter into My kingdom, when judgment day comes due (John 3:12)
I will give you hope and confidence, and tell you how to speak
You will call upon My Son, with boldness in your speech (2 Corinthians /Ephesians 3:12)
Now child strive to be perfect, though you'll never get there
For My Son, He is perfect, and your sin He did bear (Philippians 3:12)
Now I will fill your heart, with kindness and with love
And always give the same mercies; you've received from above (Colossians 3:12)
I shall show you new ways, to love each other more
The love which comes back to you, far greater than before(1Thessalonians.3:12)
My child as we take this journey, beware what lies in store
This world will try to attack you, and lead you to death once more(2Timothy 3:12)
But stand fast in My love, don't trust their wicked ways
For if the fruit I've given starts to spoil, all could rot away (Hebrew/James 3:12)
My Spirit will watch over you, I'll guide you along the way

But to them which live for evil, I'll not hear a word
thy say (1Peter 3:12)
My child, when this world has ended, and evil has
been cast down
You'll be among My precious overcomers, wearing
My victors crown (Revelation 3:12)
With guidance and love from your Creator.